A Pelican of the Wilderness

A PELICAN
of the WILDERNESS

Depression, Psalms, Ministry, and Movies

To Kettle.
Wishing you many
blessings.
Robert W. Griggs

Robert W. Griggs

CASCADE *Books* · Eugene, Oregon

A PELICAN OF THE WILDERNESS
Depression, Psalms, Ministry, and Movies

Cascade Books
An Imprint of Wipf and Stock Publishers
199 W. 8th Ave., Suite 3
Eugene, OR 97401

www.wipfandstock.com

ISBN 13: 978-1-62032-559-9

Cataloging-in-Publication data:

Griggs, Robert W.

A pelican of the wilderness : depression, psalms, ministry, and movies / Robert W. Griggs.

xiv + 164 p.; 23 cm—Includes bibliographical references

ISBN 13: 978-1-62032-559-9

1. Clergy—Mental health—United States. 2. Depression, Mental—Religious aspects—Christianity. 3. United Church of Christ—Clergy—Biography. 4. Depressed persons—United States—Biography. I. Title.

BX6495 G80 2014

Manufactured in the USA

For Susan Griggs
Wife, Nurse, Minnesotan
Without whom I would not be well.

I am like a pelican of the wilderness:
I am like an owl of the desert.

—PSALM 102:6

Contents

Introduction

IN 2006 I BECAME a patient on a locked psych unit. In the words of my admitting nurse, I had "a nasty depression." This is the story of my nasty depression, what brought me to it, and what I have taken away from it—even as I still live with it.

At the time of my hospitalization, I had served as an ordained minister of the United Church of Christ for thirty-two years. Twenty-six of these years were at the same church in Minneapolis. I was married with two grown children. I had a house, two cars, a pension, and a mental illness. As a native Virginian, I also had a well-worn book about how to speak Minnesotan.

After a fashion, I also had faith. For a long time, my faith didn't seem to be doing all that much for me one way or the other. But in my recovery, I have learned to hope in God. Without hope, I could not have gotten better. This is a story about the rebirth of hope.

The Psalms have been my bridge from despair to hope. In them, especially in the laments, I have found absolute honesty about how it feels when you hate your life. Again and again psalms tell of the terror and despair of sinking into the mire, of falling into the pit. For me, the pit and the mire are my depression and anxiety disorder. I ground my hope, my faith, on the honesty of these psalms. Their honesty about pain allows me to trust them when they speak about hope and relief from pain.

I have not been rehospitalized for depression in more than eight years. So am I well? I hope so, but only God knows. I do know that I read some psalms every day; I stay close to my family, friends, colleagues, and solid ground; and I refuse to take happiness or anything else that matters for granted. In short, I do what I've learned to do to stay well. But, like you, I live with no guarantees about my mental health or anything else.

I remember when I would lie rigid in bed with a pillow clutched tightly over my face. When I absolutely had to get up, I would stumble into the bathroom and turn on the shower to muffle the sound as I started banging my head against the shower wall. Now most mornings when the alarm goes off, I stretch out in bed like a big old cat, happy to feel good and happy for the coffee, breakfast, and sports page waiting for me in the kitchen. Maybe I even say a quick thank-you prayer before I get up. In the words of the poet Jane Kenyon, my depression has taught me how easily "it could have been otherwise."[1]

Of all the psalms that have helped me to feel good again, Psalm 40 is the one that I have called on most frequently.

> I waited patiently for the LORD; and he inclined unto me, and heard my cry.
> He brought me up also out of an horrible pit, out of the miry clay, and set my feet upon a rock, and established my goings.
> And he hath put a new song into my mouth, even praise unto our God. (Psalm 40:1–3a)

My life now is like a new song, but every day I remember the pit. A wonderful woman I met on the psych unit told me that her meltdown was the best and the worst thing that ever happened to her. This book is an affirmation of her words.

I am lucky and blessed, but I fear that I am an exception. I know for sure that my own recovery is in large measure not the work of my own hands. Without my wife and my two sons, it would not have happened. Without an array of other people, it would not have happened. I believe this as truly as I believe the Psalms.

In the hospital, I met so many people who did not have such blessings—not even close. I struggle with the unfairness of all this. It causes me to doubt the goodness and justice of God. I hurt for all those people I met in the hospital who are not loved the way that I am loved, who do not have a house, two cars, a pension, and all the rest of it. They just have the mental illness, and there is none to help, except God.

My family was the first line, but I owe my recovery to lots of people. The kindness of my admitting nurse helped me greatly during the worst hours of my life. And my first night on the psych unit, the beautiful Somali housekeeper who cleaned my hospital room with care and treated

---

1. Kenyon, *Otherwise*, 214.

me with respect gave me back a little of my dignity. If God came to me on the psych unit, God took the form of a beautiful Somali cleaning woman.

In addition, psychiatrists, therapists, friends, and parishioners have given me what I needed when I needed it. They did things for me, they told me something that I needed to hear, they just showed up. Yes, a few people along the way gave me a stone when I needed bread, but only a few.

Also I have received help from Dean Martin, Shirley MacLaine, and, best of all, Audrey Hepburn. So be honest, do you think that I've suddenly gone cuckoo again? I don't think so. Unemployed, indeed unemployable, I had lots of time in the first months of my recovery to watch old movies, often over and over again. As Cymbalta, my trusty antidepressant, has, so Turner Classic Movies has played a major role in my recovery. One of the best times that I had in the hospital was watching *Rio Bravo*, a classic John Ford Western, with a bunch of other patients.

I learned about self-respect, honesty, and other keys to recovery from watching old movies like *Rio Bravo*. I regret only that I didn't take the opportunity while we were watching *Tootsie*, another classic movie I saw on the psych unit, to throw popcorn at the screen like several of the other patients did. Who knows the next time I'll be able to toss lightly buttered popcorn at Dustin Hoffman and get away with it!

Time has passed; I have been back in ministry for seven years now. Along with the story of a nasty depression and ongoing recovery, this book is also the story of my vocation—which I sacrificed and then received again. What happened broke my heart. To borrow a phrase from Earnest Hemingway, I believe that now I am stronger in this broken place. With all the gratitude and honest humility that I can muster, I call my story a resurrection story.

In *Leaving Church: A Memoir of Faith*, Barbara Brown Taylor writes about "three distinct seasons of faith"[2] and says that Jesus called them "finding life, losing life, and finding life again."[3] In his work on the Psalms, Walter Brueggemann calls these the three seasons of orientation, disorientation, and reorientation.[4] On the church calendar, these three seasons come in one holy week. They are called Palm Sunday, Good Friday, and

---

2. Taylor, *Leaving Church*, xi.

3. Ibid.

4. Brueggemann, *The Psalms and the Life of Faith*, 9.

Easter. I've lived through these seasons, and I know that surviving what was so awful has made me stronger.

So I have this collapse, struggle, and resurrection story to tell. I believe that what I have written will be of help to anyone struggling to recover from depression, as well as to those seeking to help that person. I believe that it will be particularly helpful for anyone for whom this recovery involves a dark night of the soul, in which much is suffered and much can be learned. I believe that it will be most helpful of all to clergy like myself, men and women who have crossed the boundary between loving a congregation and trying to control a group of people, who have forgotten that all of us have a limit to the stress we can bear, and who need desperately to hear the good news that self-forgiveness is possible. (It will probably be most helpful for depressive, sixtysomething, male United Church of Christ [UCC] ministers facing a Minnesota winter, but this really limits the market.)

I recently came home from church after a twelve-hour day that ended with a meeting about planning another meeting. The commute via freeway, near the end of rush hour, took nearly an hour. At such a time, even Minnesota drivers don't practice "Minnesota nice." So what did I do? I cranked up the car radio, got the Temptations singing "My Girl," and I sang along for all I was worth. I know what it's like not to work and not to be able to work. Even a long workday can raise my spirits, especially now that my sense of irony has come back to me.

In telling my story, I try not to be pretentious or preachy, though the latter may be next to impossible for a guy who's been a preacher as long as I have. Forgive me if I make a point one too many times. It's what preachers of my generation do. Besides, these days I do my best to accept, even enjoy, who I am. At long last, I have learned that I do not need to be perfect. I am happy simply to be honest, faithful, and flawed. I've done the best I can in this book to tell the truth. I turn the results over to God.

As I said, many people have helped me. I never knew the names of some of the nurses or of my Somali housekeeper. I have chosen not to use the real names of other nurses and healthcare professionals, including my doctors and therapists, in order to avoid hampering their work. Not only do I not use the real name of my brother and sister patients on the psych unit, but I have also changed their genders, races, appearances, backgrounds, diagnoses, and ages. I have kept their confidentiality, but I can still see their faces. I offer my brothers and sisters these words:

> I had fainted, unless I had believed to see the goodness of the
> Lord in the land of the living.
> Wait on the Lord: be of good courage, and he shall strengthen
> thine heart: wait, I say, on the Lord. (Psalm 27:13–14)

Finally there are others I can thank by name, who helped save my life: Susan Griggs, Tom Griggs, David Griggs, Dr. Kirsten Schoenleber, Rev. Kathy Gibson Christensen, Rev. Tom Ewald, Rev. John Slothower, Rev. Dick Scheerer, and Rev. David Lindsay.

There are others without whom my recovery would have been slower, less complete, or less fun: Ana Orduz, Amy Bauch Griggs, Rev. Alan McNamara, Dr. Walter Griggs, Frances Griggs, Cara Griggs, Bill Lindberg, Charlie Lindberg, Jack Madson, Rev. Todd Smith Lippert, Dr. Nancy Rains Slothower, Rev. Phil Ramstad, Cindy Lemke, Dr. Gerson Sher, Margery Levine Sher, Paul Olson, Mary Kay Willert, Dr. George Chu, Eleanor Chu, Bill Thurston, Sharon Thurston, Mark Okey, Janet Okey, Jennifer Kluzak, and Andrea Peagram.

Finally I want to thank those who have helped bring this book, a project begun in the hospital, to conclusion: Jim Larson, Dr. Walter Brueggemann, Dr. Richard Crouter, Dr. K. C. Hanson, Christian Amondson, Gordeen Gorder, Jeremy Funk, Kristen Brack, and Heather Carraher.

CHAPTER 1

From Pulpit to Psych Unit

ON MY SECOND NIGHT on a locked psych unit, some of us patients got comfortable on the old sofas in front of the big TV and watched the movie *Tootsie*. We peacefully munched our popcorn from Styrofoam bowls and sipped our lemonade until some character in the movie said to Tootsie (Dustin Hoffman), "I beg you to go see a therapist."[1] Then things erupted. My fellow patients warned Tootsie not to listen to that advice. Several expressed their opinions of psychiatrists by throwing popcorn at the screen.

One big guy in his hospital-issued pajamas, robe, and tan socks with the treads on the bottom yelled, "Yeah, go see my psychiatrist. He'll send you right to the damn loony bin. He's the bastard who put me here."

A handsome middle-aged man, well-dressed except for his shoes that lacked laces, agreed, "You got that right. My therapist is crazier than I am, and that's saying a lot."

A young, thin black woman behind me chimed in, "You know what? I dare him to go see my psychiatrist. He can't say one straight sentence. I don't know where he's coming from, and I don't think he knows either. Besides, he's so damn ugly and weird. Sometimes I wonder if he's a Martian. He looks kind of green to me."

"I don't know if mine is a Martian or just a regular asshole, but he can go straight to hell."

"My psychiatrist is a Russian. He can't even speak English. How can he help me when he can't even speak our language?"

---

1. *Tootsie*, DVD, dir. Pollack.

There's not a lot of sympathy for psychiatrists on a psych unit. That's not surprising, because a pysch unit is a cemetery for psychiatrists' failures. The day before, I had been admitted because a doctor in the ER had determined I was a danger to myself. All at once, I had been sucked out of my normal life and had been dropped down into a place stranger than Oz. Yet it's where I belonged. I met all the requirements, both great and small: a life crisis with which I had failed to cope, a diagnosis of a mental illness (major depression and anxiety disorder), a plastic hospital wristband, hospital socks with treads, and a nondescript hospital room with no key.

Since I am a pastor, I could easily use the words from Genesis, "In the beginning . . . ," to start the story of how I ended up watching *Tootsie* on a psych unit. From there I could pad my story with an account of Adam and Eve, two people like me who made bad choices that played havoc with their lives. Maybe I could compare their expulsion from paradise to my own expulsion from the land of the mentally healthy. I could even identify one of my former parishioners as the snake.

From the narrative of this unfortunate couple and my parishioner (who could be much kinder now), I could add other applied Bible stories: For example, I could describe my depression as Goliath, myself as David, and my therapeutic insights as the five smooth stones David picks up for his slingshot. Were I to use another David story, my depression could this time be David, a king with some real boundary issues, and I could be the unfortunate Bathsheba, whom David is eager to pounce on. Reluctantly I will forego this analogy, leaving unexplored the intriguing gender question of why I choose to identify with Bathsheba.

Instead, I will take the Freudian route and begin with my parents. Like everybody else, I first learned how to deal with the world from my parents, who themselves were doing their best to deal with their own lives and realities. For my mom, this meant her own struggle to cope with anxiety. I remember her pacing around the living room and constantly looking out the window, unable to relax until my dad finally got home. Without words she emphatically conveyed one message to me: "Don't worry me like your dad worries me." I learned my lesson well. No matter how much I was hurting, I learned not to tell her or anybody else.

So I became an adult who played life close to the vest. I learned to deflect people with a joke or some sleight of hand so that they could never get inside. My wife, Susan, is a registered nurse whose compassion has made her the go-to person on her unit whenever a patient or family needs extra care. She would have done anything to help me. But I had learned so well how to hide my feelings that even she could not tell how much I was hurting.

As my depression deepened, I would wake in the early hours of the morning and spend the rest of the night drenched in sweat and tears, cataloging all my failures in Technicolor. Yet this was better than getting up and facing the day. When I could no longer avoid getting up, I'd tell Susan that I'd had a great night's sleep. If she said that I didn't look like I'd slept well, I'd just say I was stressed about something at work that I had to keep confidential and that next week would be easier. I could trump a lot of her concerns with an appeal to confidentiality.

From my dad I had learned other ways of coping. A self-made real-estate man, my dad drove himself hard. He was fiercely proud of all that he had accomplished. Like a character in a John Ford western movie, he lived by his own code of honor. I don't know how hard all this was for him, but I do know that one of his four siblings committed suicide and another spent her adult life in mental institutions.

Growing up, I learned to cope with my dad's pride by feeding that pride. I achieved and then achieved some more. Through my successes, I brought honor to our family name. Although he seldom said anything about my good grades or awards, I knew that my dad was proud of me. I hadn't given him any choice.

I brought these ways of coping to my work as an ordained minister. After I had served a church in New Hampshire for six years, Sue, our two little boys, and I moved to Minneapolis, where I began my ministry with a United Church of Christ congregation, not far from one of the city's famous lakes. When my meltdown happened, I was in my twenty-sixth year of service to this congregation of about three hundred members.

By the usual standards of my denomination, my pastorate was a success: budgets balanced, worship attendance up and then up some more, building projects completed, and progressive social-justice positions taken. It's fair to say that most of my colleagues respected me, and for many parishioners I had become the beloved pastor who was always there for them.

So what went wrong? To put it one way, I couldn't keep my inner dad happy. I just couldn't keep the successes coming. My church had grown, a measurable success like straight *A*'s, but the church had begun to plateau. Moreover, the growth we had obtained meant that I had more to do. With more parishioners, I just couldn't get to the hospitals every day, the nursing homes every week; I couldn't go to every school play that a child of the church was in, to every family gathering that I was invited to, to all the community events where I might meet a potential new member, and to all the rest of it. I cursed myself for slacking off and kept pushing myself to do more.

Making things still worse, I felt that I had used up all my best, even my second-best, ideas for sermons, programs, and mission events. I just wasn't doing a good job anymore. Sooner or later, probably sooner, somebody would catch on that I had become a time server, hanging around for the paychecks. I'd be weighed in the balance and found wanting. My pride couldn't stand for this to happen. I lived in fear of exposure.

In *The Noonday Demon*, Andrew Solomon, himself a depression survivor, writes that loss of an idea about oneself, a loss involving humiliation and a sense of being trapped, is responsible for triggering initial depression.[2] He goes on to say that this fear of humiliation creates terrible stress. This is what happened to me. I couldn't stand the thought that I would be found out as a phony and be ridiculed in front of my congregation. In reality this would never have happened, but I had crossed over into my own world of self-condemnation.

I tried all kinds of ways to keep the successes coming. I developed plans to add to the church staff and to enhance our youth ministry. I tried to do whatever long-term church pastors are supposed to do to keep their churches moving ahead. I looked into restructuring, reimagining, reenvisioning, reassessing, and redecorating. These are all standard ways of dealing with the realities of long tenure and a plateaued church, but I was too tired to really commit to any of them. I threw out plans like somebody tossing popcorn at a TV screen. I was just playing for time, hoping I'd feel better the next day.

Over the years I had blurred and finally erased the boundary between my church and myself. I had started to treat my church as some kind of extension of my own psyche, where I acted out my own needs and fears. I could no longer step back and take a clear look at what would actually be best for the congregation that I had been called to serve. I was unable to ask for help, unable to separate my needs from the needs of the church, unable to let go of anything: I had totally lost my way.

I remember a children's sermon where I got the youth of the church talking about what a minster does. One girl kept asking me what my real

2. Solomon, *Noonday Demon*, 63.

job was. She couldn't believe that going to church was all that I did. I don't know whatever became of her; maybe she's a therapist. Several kids said I ran the church. Did their parents nod a little too emphatically? One perceptive little boy said, "I know who you are. You are the conductor of the zoo." He nailed the way that I felt. I kept trying to control people and events like I was some kind of zookeeper or ringmaster, and it exhausted me.

I should have left. It's so clear now that my ministry in that place had run its course. All I needed to do was to declare success and seek a new call. Why didn't I do that? After all, moving on to the next call, usually one that is larger and pays better, is the standard career path for clergy.

I can live with some of the reasons I stayed and stayed: I didn't want to separate from people I had come to care deeply about, I didn't want to give up the history and trust I had built with some of these folks over more than a generation, and I didn't want to entrust their care to a stranger. Moreover, in spite of my downward spiral, there were still times I knew that by dint of my relationship with a person, I could help someone in a way no one else could. And there were some Sunday mornings when I still got it right, when my sermon helped someone experience what he or she was seeking.

There are other reasons, which aren't so noble, why I didn't want to leave. I had gotten used to a pretty good salary and long vacations. Because of his financial struggles as a young man, my dad had taught me that poverty was always a danger. We used to drive by the poorhouse in my hometown, Richmond, Virginia, and he'd say, "That's where we'll end up if your mother doesn't stop spending so much of my money." His words, his tone, still mark my attitude toward money.

Money wasn't the only fear that kept me from moving: Could I succeed in a new place? Could I find the energy to get to know and to care about an entirely new group of people? Could I actually build up another church? Would I even get another call to another pulpit? So many fears—they weighted on me like chains so that I couldn't move from that place.

In *Dakota: A Spiritual Geography*, Kathleen Norris cites a story that shows how people like me can avoid making necessary changes. Norris writes:

> One of my favorite stories . . . concerns two fourth-century monks who "spent fifty years mocking their temptations by saying, 'After this winter, we will leave here.' When the summer

came, they said, 'After this summer, we will go away from here.'
They passed all their lives in this way."[3]

In fact I liked this story so much that whenever a friend would ask
how I'd survived for so many years in the same church, I'd tell the story
to them. They'd usually laugh, but I didn't. I like dark humor, but this was
too close to home. As things closed in, I felt that I had no escapes, no
choices, and no options. I could not leave the place to which my fears had
bound me. I would just stay and hurt.

With the increasing chasm between my ways of coping and reality,
my meltdown may have been inevitable. But other factors played a role.
A few years before my hospitalization, I had badly sprained my ankle and
had to stop running: my favorite exercise. I missed the long runs that had
given me a time to let my mind float free (Zen-runner's mind). I missed
the runner's high that comes with the release of endorphins. I missed the
sense of accomplishment that comes after completing a long run. When I
ran, I was in control. And as I later learned from my psychiatrist, running
had helped me work off adrenalin and get some of the stress-inducing
hormones out of my body.

As a result of the weight gain from not being able to run, I went
on a diet. I soon lost more than twenty pounds by avoiding carbohydrates and sugar. In *The Noonday Demon*, Andrew Solomon writes, "you
can certainly bring on a depression by failing to eat the right foods."[4] By
avoiding foods with sugar and carbohydrates, I messed up my serotonin
level, which plays a key role in mental well-being.

Also Susan and I faced a very different kind of reality: we had become empty nesters. I had delighted in spending time with my children
as they grew up. When Susan worked, I got to be the primary caregiver.
What fun I had looking after my kids! (Though full disclosure warrants I
say that my sons now claim that some of the meals I served were border-
line child abuse: "Dad, it's a miracle. You've burned the ham on one end
and it's still frozen on the other.")

My sons grew up. The summer before my oldest son left for college,
I started coming home every day for lunch. He called me on it, "Dad,
how many *last suppers* are we going to have?" I grieved so hard when his
plane took off. I knew that it would never be the same again. Then a few
years later I went through the same grief when my younger son left. With

3. Norris, *Dakota*, 6.

4. Solomon, *Noonday Demon*, 138.

day-to-day parenting over, I had lost something that helped balance my work, something that I loved and could devote time to without feeling guilty.

With my failure to cope at work and my fear of humiliation growing, my depression may have been inevitable, yet these other factors certainly helped grease the skids. Then, at some point, something broke inside me, or some brain chemical gave up the ghost, or I began "to sink in deep mire" (Psalm 69:2a).

What I now know as symptoms of depression started to emerge: difficulty sleeping, the loss of interest in things that previously I had enjoyed, the inability to concentrate, and the general darkening of my mood. These were the first signs that I was sliding from transient sadness into settled depression. Tasks that used to be easy for me to get done at church became ordeals. I lost my sense of perspective so that trivial things loomed up like mountains while I ignored essentials.

My depression began to dictate my daily life. Driving to church in the morning, I would begin stopping at a coffee shop conveniently located on the way. Actually, it was a couple of blocks out of the way. I'd kill as much time as I could by sipping coffee and reading the box scores over and over. Week by week, this time that I killed drinking expensive coffee I didn't taste and reading scores I didn't remember got longer.

I also started leaving church early and spending afternoons in the back of my favorite bar, reading old *New Yorker* magazines and sipping a beer—not to get drunk, just to not be at church. Okay, to be completely honest, to get a little bit drunk, but just enough for self-medication. I never did this on days I had to go to a church meeting in the evening, though if Susan was working, I would head to the bar as soon as my meeting was over. Coffee houses and bars were my sanctuaries, better than the temple in Jerusalem.

When I was at work, I triaged. What I could postpone, I postponed. I just did not have the energy to do more than I had to; so I did the necessary, the obvious, and the public. Other tasks, like seeing people in nursing homes, or caring for those who were dealing with some kind of loss, I put off doing. This neglect of those who really needed me fed my growing feeling of self-disgust. I had become just the kind of sham minister that I loathed.

Then one day the top of my visual field disappeared. It returned, but fluctuated, as if I were having a private showing of the northern lights on the top of my eyeballs. At about the same time, a roaring started in my ears, a roaring so loud that I could only half hear. The noise became a constant, so I had to guess at what people were saying and what I was supposed to say back to them. I'm sure that if anybody had listened carefully to what I was saying, they would have been appalled.

As it all began to fall apart, I started hurting myself. One day in the shower I remembered a phone call I should have made but had forgotten. It was just a phone call, but I felt so bad that I started banging my head against the shower wall. The banging lessened the stress by creating pain that wasn't inside my head. It also punished me for becoming so incompetent and phony.

Terrified by what was happening to me, I drove around repeating over and over, "Bob, you really screwed up this time; you really screwed up this time." After a couple days of living like this, I had a nearly irresistible urge to drive into the big elm tree at the end of our block. Instead, I pulled into our driveway, opened the front door, and immediately phoned Susan. While I waited for her, I paced circles through the downstairs of our house, muttering "Oh, my God!" over and over, while totally freaking out our cat. When Susan got home, she took over and got me to the ER, thereby saving my life.

While we sat in the cubicle waiting for the doctor, I couldn't resist banging my head against the wall. I hated doing this in front of Susan— she deserved so much better than a loser like me—but I couldn't stop myself. She pleaded and held my hands. I'd stop for a few minutes until another spasm of self-loathing took over so that once again I banged my head and cursed myself.

Various hospital people came in and out of the cubicle. Most of them had plastic clipboards. One got my name wrong. The last one, who had on a long white coat, asked me some questions, found out about my family history and about my struggle not to drive into the big tree. I had said the magic words. He said, "Bob, I'm taking matters out of your hands. I'm putting you on a seventy-two-hour hold."

Soon a short, pretty woman with long brown hair and a kind voice joined us in the cubicle. She introduced herself as Sharon, the admitting nurse who would take me up to my room. Then we were joined by an obese young man with a shaved head, who was wearing a kind of quasi-police uniform. His undershirt peeked out from the gap between his last shirt button and his belt. He just stood there, chewing gum and looking bored. We were not introduced.

Then I got it. The shaved guy was there in case I made a break for it. He was the wrangler for us crazy people. Fat chance he'd catch me! If I did take off, he'd choke to death on his gum before he got me. But I had no desire or energy to escape. Leaving the ER and walking to the elevator, we formed a little procession, like the minister and the acolytes going down the aisle.

We got off the elevator, crossed a small room, and stopped in front of a green metal door. Sharon opened the door with a swipe of the plastic card on a red cord around her neck. Having wrangled me successfully, the guard left us. We entered a short hallway. Sue took my hand and held it tight. Then we came to a second door, which Sharon opened by punching a code into the lock. There was a buzz, and then the door opened. After we passed inside, she closed the door behind us, and it locked with a loud click.

We came into a large room with tables and chairs at one end and a large television with sofas in front of it at the other. There were also some easy chairs around the perimeter, as well as a fish tank. But there was no cage with small exotic birds, as you see in so many nursing homes. The room smelled like pizza that had been under a heat lamp for a long time.

Several people were sitting on the sofa watching a program, and there were a couple of people at one table playing cards. Other people were doing jigsaw puzzles, reading, or just sitting and taking it easy.

I could overhear a young woman talking loudly into one of the wall phones: "You lied to me, you son of a bitch. You told my mother I was in detox when you knew that I was here."

Several of the people were wearing exactly the same kind of pajamas.

Sharon and Susan talked awhile, and Susan told me that she had to go home to get me some things. Sharon told me that I would have my own room so that I could better, get the rest I needed. Another woman asked me lots of questions, most of which I had already answered several times in the ER. Then Sharon led me down the hall to my room. I thought she would give me a key, but there wasn't one for her to give me. After all, this wasn't a Holiday Inn.

Sharon offered to get me some herbal tea. I don't really like herbal tea, but she had been so nice that I accepted her offer, just as on a pastoral visit when someone offered me coffee and cookies I didn't want, I always smiled and took them. Better to drink bad coffee and eat stale cookies than to hurt somebody's feelings, especially somebody who might tell somebody else and start things at church going downhill for me.

Susan came back with a small suitcase. Then a nice lady—I knew that she was nice because she apologized—went through my things looking for dangerous objects. She took my belt, my disposable razor, and my dental floss. She apologized again when she said that I would have to take the laces out of my shoes and give them to her. After she had left, Susan helped me get ready for bed. Then we kissed good night and she left.

Soon someone knocked on the door. Unlike most of the people who knocked later, she actually waited for me to ask her to come in. She was a beautiful Somali woman in a long purple dress and wearing a dark orange scarf over her hair.

"Sir, may I straighten your room for you?"

When she had finished, she said, "Do not worry, sir, you will soon be home."

"Thank you," I said.

Soon after she left, a nurse came in with some pills. I took them.

The nurse must have given me some kind of ultimate sleeping pill, because soon I was asleep. I did not really fall asleep. The pill crushed me to sleep, like a stone slab falling on my brain. Several times during the night, my door opened and somebody shined a flashlight in on me. At some point a car alarm went off. It reminded me of coyotes howling. Car alarms are urban coyotes. Still, for the first time in months, I slept most of the night.

When I finally woke up, my pajamas weren't saturated with last night's sweat. How nice to wake up dry! A perky young nurse poked her head in the door and—I swear to God—asked me, "Are we feeling suicidal this morning?" I couldn't help but break out laughing, which didn't seem to daunt her. And soon, though I was still blurry-headed, the smell of French toast, bacon, and coffee perked up my nose. When was the last time that I had paid attention to smells? Or for that matter, when was the last time that I had broken out laughing?

What manner of place had I come to? Nothing in my previous life experience helped me to understand logically, emotionally, spiritually, or in any other way what had happened to me. Why like Jonah had I been coughed up on such a strange shore? What would happen to me next? What price would I be asked to pay for abandoning my old life?

Aren't Christians like me supposed to turn to faith for answers to questions like these? Aren't these the kinds of questions we are supposed to take to God in prayer? After all, I am a reverend. Yes, but spontaneous prayers stopped coming to me, and I couldn't do anything about it.

Of course for a good while I did keep on praying professionally: invocation prayers, the Lord's Prayer every Sunday, long pastoral prayers, prayers to bless the bread and wine, prayers to bless the money, closing prayers to let people know that we were finally done with church and that they could head for coffee hour. Put in a nickel, and I'd spit you out a prayer.

But spontaneous, personal prayers from my own heart had stopped coming. These are prayers like the ones that used to well up in me before I visited someone in the hospital, or like the ones that came unbidden before I preached my sermon, asking that my words would actually help those who had come to church that morning. Falling into the pit, I did only rote prayers. I needed to turn earnestly to God for help, but I was too empty, too busy, and too depressed. The prayers had stopped coming.

In *Leaving Church: A Memoir of Faith*, Barbara Brown Taylor writes about her own struggles in parish ministry: "The demands of parish ministry routinely cut me off from the resources that enabled me to do parish ministry."[5] This happened to me with prayer. It also happened with my enjoyment of Scripture. Before my depression, I used to live all week with the Scripture that I was going to preach on that Sunday. I would read commentaries and look through my theological books for connections. I would meet with lectionary groups to study the text.

And I would use a much more fun approach too: I would just mull over the Scripture, let it sink in, and live with it. Then through the week I would keep finding surprising things in the Scripture and begin to see how I could make it interesting. And since the text was on my mind, I would see events that illustrated it. The Scripture became part of me, feeding my spirit. But after my depression came, I put off sermon preparation as long as I could, and then I fought the text, trying to wring a sermon out of it. Nothing came easily or naturally. And it felt as if Sunday was coming up every other day. Scriptures that had once nourished me became just more demands on my time.

As cut off as I was from what had once sustained me, in the moment when my life hung in the balance, prayer did break through. I kept repeating, "Oh, my God!"—an urgent taking of my despair to God in prayer. My cry was akin to the prayer of the publican who smote his breast and cried, "Lord, be merciful to me a sinner" (Luke 18:13b). My prayer and the suffering from which it came is also at one with the words

---

5. Taylor, *Leaving Church*, 98.

of Jesus from the cross, "My God, my God, why hast thou forsaken me?" (Matthew 27:46b).

Here Jesus is quoting from the beginning of Psalm 22. For one tormented by depression, these words of anguish are paradoxically lifesaving words. On the lips of Jesus, as on the lips of the psalmist before him, they give biblical sanction to speaking the truth of one's unbearable pain. It is not blasphemy to ask God why you hurt so much. It is not blasphemy to tell the truth. You are not alone. Others have screamed the same questions, seeking hard comfort, but comfort nonetheless. The authors of these psalms have been there, and so has Jesus.

Other words of this psalm of lament, whatever their original intent, could have been written with the purpose of describing how my depression felt.

> But I am a worm, and no man; a reproach of men, and despised of the people.
> All they that see me laugh me to scorn: they shoot out the lip, they shake their head, saying,
> He trusted on the LORD that he would deliver him: let him deliver him, seeing he delighted in him . . .
> They gaped upon me with their mouths, as a ravening and a roaring lion.
> I am poured out like water, and all my bones are out of joint: my heart is like wax: it is melted in the midst of my bowels.
> My strength is dried up like a potsherd; and my tongue cleaveth to my jaws; and thou hast brought me into the dust of death.
> (Psalm 22:6–8, 13–15)

If I were quoting this text from the pulpit now, I would pause and then read it slowly over again to my congregation, aware that nothing I will say in response to it will equal the power of the text itself. It's all here—all the pain, terror, abandonment, and humiliation. To use a term I learned from reading the books of Walter Brueggemann about the psalms, it is a psalm of total "disorientation."[6] *Disorientation* is the word that best describes what it felt like waking up that first morning in a psych unit. I'm not in Minnesota anymore. I'm in Oz. I am totally disoriented.

Yet even in my complete disorientation, I already had a way and a fixed star. The Psalms, especially the laments, would be my way. I just didn't know it yet.

6. Brueggemann, *Message of the Psalms*, 9.

CHAPTER 2

Holy Pleasure

BEFORE I OPENED THE door of my room to go to breakfast, I double-checked to make sure all my buttons were buttoned and zippers zipped, just as I do before leaving for church on Sunday morning. There's nothing to ratchet up the anxiety like standing in the pulpit and wondering if you are zipped up. Of course pulpit robes cover a multitude of sins, but in summer it can be too hot to wear a robe. And besides, you want to be well zipped for those coffee hour conversations with visitors.

I reached into my pocket to make sure I had my keys, only to be reminded yet again of where I was. With no room key, I didn't see the point of shutting the door behind me. Venturing out into the hall, I stopped to memorize my room number, number 28: the last good year before the Great Depression.

As I walked down the hall to the social area, I kept checking over my shoulder to make sure that I could find my room again. The rooms I walked past also had their doors open and were empty. They looked the same as mine and, like me, the patients who had slept in them had not taken time to make their beds.

Going into the dining part of the social room, I half expected to see other patients holding up signs and chanting, "Look! It's Bob. Here comes the big failure." "Come see the jerk who screwed up his church. What a joke of a minister this guy is!" "This guy is a total phony and everybody knows it!"

But I saw no signs and heard no taunts. One patient did speak to me. He looked up from his own breakfast tray and the morning paper to say hi. Then he pointed me toward the cart that held the breakfast trays. I sorted through the trays and soon found the one for Robert G.

I took my tray with its plastic cover over to an empty table that had a section of the newspaper on it. I uncovered my breakfast; the smells of French toast, bacon, and coffee greeted me. I had a little trouble opening the small plastic packet of syrup and started to tense up. But I used my teeth and got the job done: a victory. Though it was a little soggier than I prefer, the French toast tasted great, and the bacon was perfect, with just the right degree of crispiness. Bacon is a forbidden pleasure at our house. The coffee was even worse than typical church-basement coffee, but it went well with the syrup and French toast. I cleaned my plate; I'm sure I ate more breakfast than I had eaten all the mornings of the previous month put together.

I walked over to the counter in front of the nurses' station and got a second cup of the not-so-good coffee. Full and satisfied, I looked around the room as I sipped my coffee. Some of the other patients were fully dressed like me—if you can be fully dressed with no belt or shoelaces—while others were wearing robes over pajamas. Some had already finished breakfast and were watching TV, talking on one of the wall phones, visiting, or just sitting looking at nothing in particular.

I turned to the newspaper and started by reading *Mark Trail* in the comic section. Some drug smugglers had left him and his square jaw to die in the middle of the ocean. Sharks swam closer and closer. Not to worry, Mark would get out of this tight spot, just as he had gotten out of all the others. The bad guys would pay; justice would be done. All else may pass away, but you can count on Mark Trail. Next I read the sports section: a win for the Minnesota Timberwolves basketball team, with Kevin Garnett scoring twenty-four points: KG, another guy you can count on.

Give or take a few details, the whole scene was so normal that I could have been eating breakfast at a cheap restaurant—one that allowed customers to come in their pj's and, better yet, one that didn't bring you the check when you were done eating. Less than a day earlier, I had been banging my head against the ER wall, and now I was sipping my coffee, reading my paper, and checking things out. Go figure.

I realized the one thing that I was not doing: running scenarios in my head about church: about who had missed a couple Sundays in a row, about who had said what at the deacons' meeting, about the lack of any visitors the last couple weeks, about the price of electricity, about the cost of boiler repairs, about exhausting the snow-removal budget by mid-December in Minnesota, about getting a teacher for the junior-high

Sunday school class, about getting delegates for the next state denominational meeting, about the Alcoholics Anonymous group member who
had parked in front of a neighbor's driveway, about the cranky computer,
about the drop in the church's investment account, about a bylaws-review
committee gone rogue, about the gentle-yoga group that hadn't paid its
rent, about the alleged bat sighting in the second-grade Sunday school
classroom, about who in my congregation would be offended if I spoke
up more directly about all the reasons we should not be in Iraq, and so
on.

On the way back to my room, number 28, I stopped to pick up some
flyers from the counter at the nurses' station. They listed various depression support groups in the Twin Cities. As I had hoped, the backs of the
flyers were blank. Next to the stack of flyers stood a coffee mug (adver-
tising some drug that I had never heard of) full of yellow mechanical
pencils. The aide or secretary told me that the pencils were for patient
use. I splurged and took two.

Back in my room, I kind of made up the bed. I sat down on it and
tried to figure out how to work the pencil. I just couldn't get the lead
out. Maybe all the lead had been used up, but it looked new; the eraser
was unused. The more I messed with it, the more frustrated I got. I can't
even work a damn pencil. That's it. I am an absolute incompetent in every
conceivable way. I almost threw the damn mechanical pencil against the
wall. Then by accident, I turned the tip of the pencil and suddenly lead
appeared: another small victory. I practiced until I was certain that I had
mastered the pencil.

I lay back on the bed and used the blank areas of the pamphlets to
record my impressions of the previous twenty-four hours or so. I had
journaled regularly for decades, until my depression had gotten bad.
Then I lost the energy for it; besides there was nothing in my life worth
writing down. For me, who used to record all the day's highlights, not
journaling was a way of committing daily minisuicides. That morning,
fueled by French toast and bacon, I had lots of things that I wanted to
write down. Journaling can be a step in getting perspective. You choose
to write down what you think is important and omit the rest. You're in
control. Besides, for me anyway, I like to write. It makes me happy.

Living my first good day in a long time, I was content to let things
be, but the hospital staff had other ideas. For them, I needed to get a
move on, so they decided to give me a jump-start. Soon after lunch, a

nurse came to give me some Ritalin. I asked her why, and she said that for adults Ritalin increases activity.

Did it ever! After a little while the Ritalin exploded in my head—sky rockets in flight! Increased activity? I could have run back-to-back marathons; preached to vast, hostile multitudes; climbed Mount Everest while holding my breath. Here's a thought, which I owe (at least in part) to Garrison Keillor: if you spiked the communion wine with Ritalin, then would the whole congregation have the strength to get up and do what needs to be done?

Gradually the Ritalin high smoothed down, but I stayed pumped up for the rest of the day. I had the energy to do some reading, another pleasure that I had lost to depression. I sat down in the social room and started reading a science-fiction novel about whales, *Fluke: Or, I Know Why the Winged Whale Sings* by Christopher Moore, a man who had also written a comic life of Jesus. Sue had grabbed it when she packed my bag.

Sitting in a psych unit, listening to a voice over the public-address system paging Dr. Blue, and reading about whale songs—I half expected the Munchkins to come marching through the door. *Fluke* fit right into my new life on the far side of the yellow brick road. In it a ganja-smoking character describes a break-in and subsequent vandalism in a whale research center as "a bit of fuckery most heinous."[1] On reading that, I laughed out loud. Depression surely had wrought some fuckery most heinous into my own life.

After a while another patient came and sat down beside me. She didn't have anything to read, didn't say anything to me. She started rocking rhythmically back and forth. I thought she must really be out of it. When she got up and went to the nurses' station, I saw that there was a good reason that she had been rocking back and forth. The chair next to me was a rocking chair. As in Scripture, so on a psych unit: judge not.

She came back with a Styrofoam bowl full of mixed nuts and offered me some. Of course I took a handful and thanked her politely. "They keep these at the desk for me," she explained. "They come in a glass bottle, and I can't have that. It's inconvenient, but those are the rules."

A thin woman with sharp features, probably somewhere in her early sixties, she introduced herself as Anna. We ate nuts and told each other our breakdown stories. She suffered from depression and lived alone. For

1. Moore, *Fluke*, 20.

her, the tipping point had come when bill collectors obtained her cell-phone number and started harassing her.

She told me, "I pray that I can die, but God doesn't listen. I just don't want to go on living. It hurts too bad. I lie in bed, watch the hands on my clock, and want to die. I'm too tired to kill myself, but I could have just stayed in bed and starved to death. But my social worker got worried when she couldn't get me on the phone and came to my apartment. She has a key. That's how I ended up here. In the emergency room, they asked me about my mood. I told them that I was too tired to have any moods."

We talked until all the nuts were gone, and then she went to take a nap. That night we ended up having supper with two other patients. They also became friends. Like the medical staff, Anna and my other new friends assisted in my recovery. I've often wondered if the professionals are aware of how much patients can help one another, not only in group therapy, but also just by hanging out together on the unit. At any rate, Anna taught me many things. I especially prize what she said about pleasure: "I took pleasure for granted. That was my big mistake. Take your eye off pleasure, and you will lose it."

I had taken my eye off pleasure and lost it. But I was learning that I had not lost it forever. You can get pleasure back again: have a good night's sleep, even if it's drug induced; have bacon and French toast for breakfast; journal, if you like to write; eat nuts with a wise stranger. I think back to the question from my ultraperky, patronizing yet wonderful nurse: "Are we feeling suicidal this morning?" I didn't think that anybody could ever make me laugh again, but she had cracked me up my first morning on the psych unit.

I only wish that instead of answering her just no, I had said, "No, we don't feel suicidal this morning. And no offense intended, but, please, tell me, can we do perky 24/7? And one more thing, are you Sandra Dee's little sister, by any chance?"

Of all the reasons for living that have returned to me since my depression, pleasure came back first. Pleasure is tough and resilient. Other reasons for living had to wait until I could think clearly again or could just stay calm. But pleasure came back with the bacon. Every time I read the following part of Psalm 30, I thank God for the return of pleasure.

> O LORD my God, I cried unto thee, and thou hast healed me.
> O LORD, thou hast brought up my soul from the grave: thou hast
> kept me alive, that I should not go down into the pit.

> Sing unto the LORD, O ye saints of his, and give thanks at the remembrance of his holiness.
>
> For his anger endureth but a moment; in his favor is life: weeping may endure for a night, but joy cometh in the morning. (Psalm 30:2–5)

The first part of this quote ("the grave" and "the pit") is real to my experience of falling into depression. As the psalmist did, I cried out in pain because I could not endure it; however, I had no choice other than suicide but to endure it. And though I didn't cry out directly to God, I did make a phone call that I am convinced saved my life. God has "kept me alive" by proxy. The second part of the quote ("joy cometh in the morning") is also real to my experience, as real to me as the smell of bacon. To recover my mental health, I needed to recover joy in things both great and small. I needed to recover a lot else, but joy turned out to be my starting place.

Theologians make distinctions between *joy, pleasure, happiness,* and other allied terms: pleasure passes while joy endures—that sort of thing. But for my purposes, I will use these terms largely interchangeably as referring to whatever it is—maybe the smell of bacon, maybe the sunshine, maybe the prospect of meaningful work—that makes one want to get out of bed and live another day.

In *The Noonday Demon*, Andrew Solomon writes about depression. "The first thing that goes is happiness. You cannot gain pleasure from anything. That's famously the cardinal symptom of major depression."[2] You first lose the joy that "cometh in the morning," as I had done many months before my hospitalization.

Yet there I was less than twenty-four hours after my admission, no longer pounding my head against the wall, but exhibiting unmistakable symptoms of happiness. Yes, pleasure can be as tough as a church treasurer, but why, and in a psych unit of all places, did it suddenly come back to me? How is this possible?

Psalm 23 helps one to answer these questions. This psalm is not a lament, but it offers what many in the laments are seeking: "Thou preparest a table before me in the presence of mine enemies: thou anointest my head with oil; my cup runneth over" (Psalm 23:5). This is a vision of sanctuary; the enemies are still there, but you are in a safe place. They can look, but they can't touch.

2. Solomon, *Noonday Demon*, 19.

My enemies included all the demands that I had heaped upon my own head, and all the self-accusing thoughts that swarmed in my mind. I had tried to find sanctuary from them in a coffee shop and a bar. I needed some place safer, a place where fear would not cut me off from pleasure. I didn't know it at the time, but I was like the hart in Psalm 42.

> As the hart panteth after the water brooks, so panteth my soul after thee, O God.
> My soul thirsteth for God, for the living God: when shall I come and appear before God?
> My tears have been my meat day and night, while they continually say unto me, Where is thy God?
> When I remember these things, I pour out my soul in me: for I had gone with the multitude, I went with them to the house of God, with the voice of joy and praise, with a multitude that kept holyday. (Psalm 42:1–4)

The "water brooks" and the "house of God" are places of sanctuary. In body and soul I was panting for such a place where I could be safe from my parishioners. In my mind, they were pursuing me relentlessly, exhausting me in the chase. My parishioners had become my enemies.

This is how I felt. It has little to do with my parishioners in reality. In reality, many of these parishioners would have made large sacrifices to make me happy. But I could not tell them how unhappy I had become. So I needed a safe place, and I needed it right now. So did the other patients in the psych unit. We all needed sanctuary from overwhelming demands, fears, losses, and troubles of all kinds, including bill collectors and parishioners.

In reality the achievement of sanctuary is one of the collateral benefits of hitting bottom and landing in a psych unit. You can't get out, but they can't get in. You can eat and drink in safety, mocking your enemies, laughing at the devil. And best of all, neither the devil nor one of your parishioners can call you.

At home I dreaded phone calls, especially calls in the evening. Just the thought that the phone might ring was enough to keep me tense when I needed to relax. With the click of the lock on the unit's door, the phone had lost its power. The odds of a parishioner calling me were very long. And if by chance one did, I'm sure that they would have hung up as soon as the secretary said, "Hello. Loony bin. How may I direct your call?"

By objective standards, my life had hit bottom. On the day that I was admitted, my freedom had been taken from me. I could not even control who came in and out of my room, or what the medications I was given were doing to my mind. Whatever a successful life is, this is surely not it; put "spent time in the psych unit" on your résumé and see if it helps get you a job. For someone as proud as I am and so in need of success, I had landed in the hell that would seem to have been designed especially for me.

And yet I found pleasure. Hitting bottom had not turned out to be all that bad. It was certainly a couple of steps up from the hell that I had been living in for some time. Safe and free from demands, I had laid my burden down, as the spiritual says. I had traded freedom for safety, control for sweet surrender, and I had ended up a winner. I had been forced to let go and let God. I didn't know yet what God might do, but the letting go and accepting sanctuary had turned out to be wonderful. Pleasure had returned. "O taste and see that the LORD is good" (Psalm 34:8a).

Since my hospitalization I've tried my best never to take pleasure for granted and to follow Anna's admonition to keep my eye on it. I have experienced that much of pleasure is anticipation, like the smell of bacon announcing the pleasure of a good meal. I believe that anticipatory pleasure is the genesis of hoping, making hope as real as your favorite smell. Maybe something like this was in the mind of the author of Psalm 30: one can endure the weeping that lasts for a night if one anticipates the joy that comes in the morning. Otherwise, you might as well stay in bed with a pillow over your head. Stay in bed long enough, as Anna wanted to do, and you'll just die.

My recovery has taught me that I needed to relearn how to enjoy the taste of a strip of bacon before I could relearn how to enjoy all the pleasures of listening to good music, and that I needed to have a casual conversation with a stranger before I could reexperience the full delight of being the pastor of a congregation and living in a maze of relationships. Recovery takes time—one day at a time, one pleasure at a time.

Moving from simple to complex pleasures, one begins a journey that can indeed lead one to say, "O taste and see that the LORD is good." In *Reflections on the Psalms*, C. S. Lewis writes, "I want to stress what I think that we (or at least I) need more; the joy and delight in God which meet us in the Psalms."[3] Perhaps noticing "the joy and delight in God" is a learned skill, as some writers say that faith is. In which case, one can start the journey toward tasting the goodness of God with a good

3. Lewis, *Reflections*, 50.

breakfast—bacon or perhaps something a little healthier, as long as it smells and tastes good.

This point can be made in a different way. Above I wrote about anticipatory pleasure as the genesis of hoping. This also has implications for one's journey to God. As Eugene H. Peterson writes about Psalm 13 in *Answering God: The Psalms as Tools for Prayer*, "The prayer, for a moment, is in touch with its final end, its completion is praise. 'Most joy is anticipatory,' says Karl Barth. 'It normally has something of an eschatological character.'"[4] Doesn't this mean, at least in part, that experiencing life's pleasures is also practice for life in the kingdom of God, where there will be joy without end and pleasure for evermore?

Today I savor the daily pleasures of food, company, and entertainment. Stretching out in bed under clean sheets, knowing I will be able to fall asleep and wake up refreshed, makes me want to go to bed. Anticipating a mug of freshly ground coffee, maybe next to a hot English muffin, one with all those little whorls and caves glistening with butter, makes me want to get up in the morning. I've learned not to despise the daily pleasures. I hold each one as a gift of God.

Psalm 104, a hymn of praise to God for the vastness and goodness of creation, also celebrates some of life's small pleasures and little blessings.

> He causeth the grass to grow for the cattle, and herb for the service of man: that he may bring forth food out of the earth;
> And wine that maketh glad the heart of man, and oil to make his face to shine, and bread which strengtheneth man's heart.
> (Psalm 104:14–15)

Herbs and bread may be necessary for life, though some crusty rosemary bread dipped in genuine extra-virgin olive oil also rates high on the pleasure scale. But wine, whatever its collateral cardiac benefits, is intended by God to make us glad. In moderation, wine and its fermented cousins are daily pleasures. And oil in biblical days kept the skin supple against the heat and wind of an arid land while also giving the skin a healthy glow. If that same oil were scented, then it would have delighted the sense of smell, the sweet perfume of God.

"Thou anointest my head with oil; my cup runneth over" (Psalm 23:5b). These words from Psalm 23 about sanctuary also celebrate God as the source of life's pleasures. They tell us that God is not stingy. God doesn't just give us a sip of wine; our cups overflow; and I'm sure that

---

4. Peterson, *Answering God*, 123–24.

they overflow with a good vintage, though probably not as good as the one created by Jesus when he turned six water pots, containing two or three firkins of water apiece, into wine at the wedding at Cana in Galilee. Using standard firkin equivalencies, this easily could have been over 125 gallons of Zagat—top-rated wine! Selfishness is a human invention. In creating life and in giving pleasure to us creatures, God is abundant, even profligate.

Hence we have the words of doxology: "Praise God from whom all blessings flow." And hymns like "Come, Thou Fount of Every Blessing." And Psalm 23 isn't the only psalm that speaks of God's abundance. It is a recurring theme of the psalms: "Thou wilt shew me the path of life: in thy presence is fulness of joy: at thy right hand there are pleasures for evermore" (Psalm 16:11). "Thou shalt make them drink of the rivers of thy pleasures" (Psalm 36:8b). "Thou openest thine hand, and satisfieth the desire of every living thing" (Psalm 145:16; see also Psalm 104:28). "Who satisfieth thy mouth with good things; so that thy youth is renewed like the eagle's" (Psalm 103:5).

In his meditation on the book of Ecclesiastes, *When All You've Ever Wanted Isn't Enough*, Rabbi Harold Kushner shares with his readers what he calls "one of the most profound religious thoughts I know."[5] It's a passage from the Talmud, a book he describes as "the collected wisdom of the rabbis of the first five centuries."[6] The Talmud has this to say about enjoyment of pleasure: "In the world to come, each of us will be called to account for all the good things that God put on earth which we refused to enjoy."[7] In other words, in the world to come, we will be called to account for all the pleasures that we chose to turn away from.

This is startling and wonderful in its implications. Christians have been taught that we will be held accountable for the sins that we commit. Now we learn that we will also be held accountable for the pleasures that we omit, for all the good things of God that we refuse to enjoy. Then again, following the Talmud maybe this very refusal to enjoy God's good things is a sin, so that it's a sin to neglect to enjoy a sunset, to fail to take time to really listen to a piece of music, or to refuse even a little taste of dark chocolate now and again. If so, I've been repenting and amending my way of life for some time now, enjoying the good things of life as

5. Kushner, *When All You've Ever Wanted*, 82.
6. Ibid.
7. Ibid.

much as I can or can afford. I invite you to join me. Glasses of wine in hand, let's have a good time getting ready for the Judgment Day.

Rabbi Kushner draws attention to a passage in Ecclesiastes that tells us enjoying the good things of life is not to be postponed. This is his translation.

> Go, eat your bread in gladness and drink your wine in joy, for your action was long ago approved by God. Let your clothes always be freshly washed and your head never lack ointment. Enjoy happiness with a woman you love all the fleeting days of life that have been granted you under the sun. Whatever it is in your power to do, do it with all your might. For there is no doing, no learning, no wisdom in the grave where you are going. (Ecclessiastes 9:7–10)[8]

In this passage, the realization of our mortality adds urgency to the enjoyment of life's pleasures. This could be depressing news, of course, making the enjoyment of small pleasures yet another of the things that are fleeting, one of the "vanities" decried by the author of Ecclesiastes. But it needn't be depressing, and it has not been depressing for me in my recovery. It is, rather, a warning against procrastinating in the face of pleasure; you must enjoy the good things of this life while you still can. Don't let your ice cream melt or flies get on your pie. If you procrastinate too long, all the rhubarb will have gone to seed. Again Anna is right: keep your eye on pleasure, or you will lose it.

There is so much I regret about the time I lost to depression, including all the pleasures I let go by—pleasures both great and small. I regret as well the pleasure that my depression cost the people who love me. Never again will I let this happen. Enjoying the many pleasures of life, we honor God the giver, and take in that which will sustain us when troubles come. Through pleasure we create a bulwark for ourselves against depression. Never, never despise pleasure or take it for granted.

This point is amplified by Morrie Schwartz in the book *Tuesdays with Morrie* by Mitch Albom. As Morrie is dying of ALS, Lou Gehrig's disease, Albom is given the honor of visiting with him and recording his reflections and wisdom in the face of physical decline and death. Morrie is our teacher in what it means to enjoy the good things of life, especially small pleasures, while being always aware that one does not have unlimited time to enjoy them.

8. Ibid., 140.

One exchange between Mitch and Morrie is especially telling:

> He [Morrie] nodded toward the window with the sunshine streaming in. "You see that? You can go out there, outside, anytime. You can run up and down the block and go crazy. I can't do that. I can't go out. I can't run. I can't be out there without fear of getting sick. But you know what? I *appreciate* that window more than you do."
>
> "Appreciate it?"
>
> "Yes. I look out that window every day. I notice the change in the trees, how strong the wind is blowing. It's as if I can see time actually passing through that windowpane. Because I know my time is almost done, I am drawn to nature like I'm seeing it for the first time."[9]

Reading this, I am reminded of something else that Anna told me: "Bob, my meltdown was the worst thing and the best thing that ever happened to me." Why it is the worst thing is easy enough to discern. But the best thing? In part, I believe, it is because the meltdown taught her, as it has taught me, not to take pleasure for granted. Pleasure is so easy to find—just look out the window and really see what's there. But when your mind is so troubled, pleasure is also easy to lose.

At the edge of death, Morrie found pleasure in looking out a window. On a psych unit, I found pleasure in breakfast, a movie, a conversation. These are little things, easily taken for granted and easily lost. I am one of the lucky ones. Though I lost them, I have gotten them back again. I have met a lot of people who have found their lost pleasure. I met them on the unit, at church, and in the Psalms.

This talk about pleasure raises for me a personal question, which is also a bit of a mental and geographical digression. If I value pleasure so passionately, and truly recognize that it can so easily be lost, why do I live in Minnesota, of all places? After all, Minnesota is the state where it is alleged that winter is only broken by a brief mosquito-swatting season. It is where cream peas on white toast is soul food. And as has been rumored, it is also where the consumption of lutefisk—cod preserved in lye, washed repeatedly, and then often overcooked so that it is served as fish jelly—is a sacrament, not to be enjoyed but endured.

In reality one can find much pleasure even here in Minnesota. I actually like "roast pork commercial," a delicacy of western Minnesota, available near the town of Benson. It's white meat on Wonder Bread,

9. Albom, *Tuesdays with Morrie*, 84.

topped with a pound or so of mashed potatoes, all smothered in white gravy. Though lutefisk is wretched (I have just cost myself the possibility of employment in a host of Scandinavian-background churches), torsk ("poor man's lobster") is delicious, lefse is good, and the desserts—krumkake, rosettes, rommegrot, kringle, flan, rice pudding and lingonberries, rhubarb-and-strawberry pie—almost compensate for the lutefisk.

Furthermore, in a land where windchill can drop faster than the stock market, it is nevertheless true that simply stepping in from the cold is a great pleasure. And after you scrape the frost off your glasses, you can enjoy the crackling fire in the fireplace. However, I have to admit that this particular pleasure does feel a little too much like the pleasure of stopping after you've been hitting your head against a wall.

In truth, pleasure is mutable and diverse, always surprising us by where and when it is found. We rugged Minnesotans don't have warm beaches shaded with palm trees, but we do have winter days when the bright sun shines on the fresh snow and one tingles with energy. One can just look out the window and enjoy it—or better, go out and build a snowman.

And in the summer, people here do talk about going to "the lake," without naming which lake—because we have so many. We have the northern lights and summer twilights that go on for hours. And as for food, why eat cream peas on toast when our recent immigrants from all over the world have opened restaurants that can set your taste buds jumping for joy?

I hope that I have satisfied those who think that it's odd, maybe even a little hypocritical, for a Minnesotan to rhapsodize about pleasure. I want to close this digression with a plea for what I call pleasure tolerance. If somebody wants to eat cream peas on toast or fish jelly, if they do not force others to do the same, and if they are willing to do it in the privacy of their own homes, what's the problem? There is no accounting for taste or for pleasure.

A scene in a movie celebrates this enjoyment of small pleasures. It takes us away from Minnesota to the pleasures of Manhattan. Moreover, since it involves Audrey Hepburn, it gives us the enjoyment of beauty, another pleasure that is never to be taken for granted.

At the beginning of *Breakfast at Tiffany's*, a taxi pulls up in front of Tiffany's, the grand jewelry store. It's already light, but too early in the morning for there to be any traffic. The young woman who gets out of the taxi, Holly Golightly (Audrey Hepburn), obviously has had a long night. She is wearing a long, slightly crumpled black evening gown, long black gloves, large sunglasses, and diamonds, be they real or fake. Holding a doughnut and a cup of coffee, she stands there staring into the store window, which reflects her gaze. Then she bites the doughnut to free her hands so that she can pop off the lid of her cup of coffee. She is ready for breakfast at Tiffany's.

Whenever I want to remember how important it is to respect the little joys of life, how large a role they play in my recovery, I come back to this scene and remember Audrey Hepburn, the picture of elegance, munching away in front of Tiffany's. I can even hear in my mind the Henry Mancini background music "Moon River" playing as she looks, sips, and eats.

Later on in the movie, we learn all that Tiffany's means to her. Sometimes she gets what she calls the "mean reds."[10] She says the mean reds are horrible: "Suddenly you are afraid and don't know what you're afraid of."[11] When this happens, she takes a cab and heads for Tiffany's.

> It calms me down right away, the quietness and the proud look of it. Nothing very bad could happen to you there. If I could find a real-life place that makes me feel like Tiffany's, then I'd buy some furniture and give the cat a name.[12]

It turns out that she really doesn't need a lot to beat the mean reds—which is an apt way of describing anxiety disorder. Breakfast at Tiffany's, just a little pleasure, is sufficient to send the mean reds packing. Holly has a lot to learn, but she already knows a lot about herself. She realizes that if somehow she could sustain this pleasure by finding a place that feels like Tiffany's, her sanctuary, then she could settle down. To Holly, giving the cat a name symbolizes getting on with her life.

What I learned on a psych unit, Holly learned in front of Tiffany's: pleasure and sanctuary go together. After much struggle and many near misses, Holly also learns that a sanctuary need not be a place. The best sanctuary can be another person. In faith terms, the same lesson is in the Psalms, such as in Psalm 25, where this "person" is God: "O my God, I trust in thee" (Psalm 25:2a). For people of faith, the presence of God is the ultimate sanctuary. God, the one from whom all blessings flow, is also

10. *Breakfast at Tiffany's*, DVD, dir. Edwards.
11. Ibid.
12. Ibid.

the one who will keep us safe so that we can enjoy these blessings and drink from this river of pleasures.

In her popular memoir *Eat, Pray, Love*, Elizabeth Gilbert tells about her travel to Italy in pursuit of a different kind of pleasure: the food, the warmth, the people, the delight of speaking the language itself. In good measure her striving to recover from depression motivates her pursuit of pleasure. She has learned, as I have, the importance of pleasure in restoring one's mental health.

On a visit to Sicily, she muses on how Sicilians live well in a world of disorder and disaster. She finds the answer in their appreciation and respect for the gift of pleasure.

> Still I will say that the same thing which has helped generations of Sicilians hold their dignity has helped me begin to recover mine—namely, the idea that the appreciation of pleasure can be an anchor of one's humanity.[13]

Of all that might anchor one's humanity in reality, pleasure is the most neglected. Maybe that's why depression is epidemic in our culture. We have been sold sham pleasures and taught to labor for that which cannot satisfy our bodies, let alone bring us to God. However that may be, I am certain that the recovery of pleasure is critical to recovery from depression. Moreover, as Holly, Elizabeth, and I can all tell you in our different ways, it's so easy: all you need to do is take that first bite.

13. Gilbert, *Eat, Pray, Love*, 115.

CHAPTER 3

Laments

I FOUND PLEASURE ON a psych unit in the midst of a lot of pain. Having acknowledged the importance of pleasure and seen how pleasure can help to heal heart and soul, I found it necessary again to face up to the reality of pain. As the authors of the laments knew long ago, only in this way can one finally leave the pain behind.

At times on the unit, the pain of another patient burst out with no warning. One morning while I was sitting in the social room sipping coffee and reading the paper, a young woman with beautiful long black hair suddenly collapsed in front of the nurses' desk. I don't know what happened, but suddenly she was lying on the floor screaming, "Help me! Help me! They can't do this to me! Help me! Help me! O God, won't somebody please help me! Make them stop! O God, make them stop!" Gently a nurse helped her up and led her away. I never saw her again.

Over breakfast the next day, I talked with an African American man who had a great gift of storytelling, including an absolutely impeccable sense of timing. He told me about a domestic dispute involving his parents when he was six or seven. "The funniest part was after the cops arrived. They handcuffed my dad and started to take him out the door. My mom was screaming all to beat hell. Then she turned around and slugged my dad in the mouth as hard as she could. Shit! That's what she did. He started to bleed all over the place. You know what the cops did? They took the handcuffs off my dad and put them on my mom. I swear to God that's what happened." Funny? Sure. Especially how he told it. But if you think about it from a little boy's perspective, it can break your heart.

Our group-therapy work was all about pain and what to do with it. I began going to therapy groups my second day on the unit. The first day a nurse had told me that the staff thought I needed a day to just relax before I began group work. That was fine with me, especially as it had turned out to be such a good day. When another patient asked me why I had not been in group, I told him, "I didn't go to group because they told me that I was too depressed for the depression group." Like any preacher working up a sermon illustration, I had massaged what the nurse had told me to make a better story.

At 10 a.m. my second day in the hospital, I went to my first group, part of the psych unit's Crisis Management Program (CMP). All the handouts I have from that time give the full name of the group, followed by the initials *CMP*. Still, I never heard anybody call the sessions anything but "group." I wondered what those initials were about. Could it be that whoever wrote the handouts hoped that using the initials *CMP* would make the group feel more comfortable, more familiar to us? Like, "I'm really fine, just here for a little CMP. You know, R&R, TLC"—that sort of thing. "Whatever," as we say in Minnesota.

We had three CMP groups, which mixed together patients from the three psych units in the hospital. Most of the patients in my group seemed to be suffering from depression or bipolar disorder. A number of us also had chemical-dependency issues.

We met in a windowless green room with over-bright fluorescent lights. The chairs were all wheeled office chairs, the kind often on sale at Office Depot. A blank whiteboard hung on one wall and a picture of a garden in full spring hung on another, a marked contrast to the below-freezing weather outside. An upright piano and a piano bench were jammed against the far wall. The calendar on the wall was a day late; the wall phone lacked a receiver. As people came in, they invariably sat in alternating chairs, until folks had to start filling in. In all there were eight of us.

Eric, the staff member who led the group, looked to be in his late thirties. He had black hair that fell over his eyes. With his brown corduroys and dark green turtleneck, he looked like the kind of guy that you see in Starbuck's sipping a latte and reading a book on advanced pottery. In the book of Isaiah, God is a potter; so, good for Eric. Maybe he could shape us into something better.

He started by asking each of us to introduce ourselves and to give a report on the progress that we had made on yesterday's goals. Immediately I tensed up because I didn't have anything to report. I always did my homework and double-checked to make sure that I had it with me.

Would Eric be mad with me? Of course, logically there was no way he could have expected me to do an assignment that I knew nothing about. But I had landed in Oz, and logic did not apply.

Things moved along until we got to the guy sitting on my left. "I'm Jack," he said. "Otherwise I'm not telling you a damn thing. I don't trust anybody here, and I have good reason not to trust you. And, oh yes, I wasn't in group yesterday, but my goal for today is to learn to be more assertive. How am I doing so far?"

I wondered how Eric the potter was going to handle Jack. Jack looked like a guy who worked out a lot or maybe had a job that required lots of heavy lifting. He rocked back and forth, stopping only when he spoke. Though he seemed very tired, he was a handsome young man, tattoos and all.

For so many years in ministry, I had tried to make people get along, to prevent conflicts if possible, or to quickly resolve them when they arose. I always took conflict to be my responsibility; I never accepted that something good might come out of conflict or even that some people might enjoy it.

Now here I was close to a guy who seemed about to explode. Shouldn't I do something? As my stomach clutched and my breathing sped up, I struggled not to say anything. This wasn't a church meeting, and nobody expected me to smooth things over and head off conflict. Of course, even at church, I was the only person who expected me always to do this. I had learned my lessons too well as a child: don't upset Mom, avoid Dad's anger, and thereby keep everybody happy.

"Jack," Eric said slowly, "I want to respect where you're coming from, but can you tell us why you're feeling the way that you are?"

"Because I know about you guys. I know this is the way you make your money. The only reason I came here to group was I knew if I didn't, you'd put it in my file that I was noncooperative. I'm probably already in trouble for not coming here yesterday. But you people put me on Seconal, and I was too drugged to come. So I'm here today, and I don't choose to say anything about myself. But don't worry. I won't take a swing at anybody."

As Jack went on, I kept rolling my chair further away from him.

Eric accepted what Jack had to say, and check-in went on. Then Eric asked which of us wanted time to speak in group. I volunteered, along with three other patients. I volunteered because I thought it would please Eric, the one in authority, the one whose approval I wanted. Sometimes

I react against this side of myself. But under stress, this time I chose to please.

When Jack mentioned a file, I thought, "report card." So another reason I volunteered to talk in group was to get the therapy-group equivalent of good grades. Surely you got credit for class participation. Good grades would help me to be discharged sooner. Being discharged meant that I had succeeded: maybe I could even get *magna cum laude* on my discharge papers.

I went first in group and told my story as accurately as I could. Once I began, I didn't think about pleasing Eric or angering Jack. It all came pouring out. I told them how I had let everybody in my church down and how angry I was at myself. I just put it all out there: my being a minister, the pain I felt in my work, the head banging, the almost-swerving into a tree—all of it. When I was done telling my meltdown story, I started to tremble. I hadn't meant to say so much or reveal so much. I started to shiver, and I hugged myself to get warm.

Several group members rushed to reassure me. Dottie, who had multiple scars on her forehead and a large unicorn tattooed on her shoulder, told me, "It must take a lot of courage, you being a reverend and all, to admit you have a problem and come in here and be with us loonies." Another woman, still dressed in her pajamas and a robe, leaned toward me and said, "You know a jerk can be a preacher as soon as he can be anything else. But you don't laud it over us like God Almighty."

"Bob," Eric said, "I know that you're hurting now. It's hard for you to see anything positive. But you served your church—for what?—over a quarter of a century. It will take time, but I believe that you will be able to see all the good that you have done. You will feel better. We'll work together on recognizing reality and radical self-acceptance."

"Thanks. Maybe I have done some good. But I don't feel that way now. I've been faking it, just getting by, only doing what I had to. I hate myself for being such a phony. I just can't face it anymore. I'm supposed to be able to help other people, and I can't even help myself."

Dottie said, "I'm glad you're here. I've never heard a minister talk about himself before. I thought reverends weren't real people. But you're human like the rest of us."

Eric asked me if it was okay for the group to move on. Lydia spoke next. She was a heavy young woman whose pale complexion contrasted with her bright red lipstick. She wore pajama pants and a large pink

T-shirt with a white kitten on it. As she spoke, she twisted a wad of tissue in her lap.

She told us that she had been living alone with her baby. She used to live with her boyfriend, the baby's father, but he had moved out when she told him that she was pregnant and refused to get an abortion. "I've failed totally as a mother," she sobbed. "My son is only six weeks old. I'm so scared that I will hurt him. He cries all the time, and I can't get him to stop. I'm scared of my own baby. I was so afraid of hurting him that I took him to my mom's house and checked in here. My mom and the baby are supposed to come today. I'm afraid to see him. I know that I won't stop crying."

Eric made eye contact with her. "Lydia, a lot of women with postpartum depression are afraid they'll say or do something to hurt their child. It's a terrible tension. You'll get help here with your medications and therapy. And you will feel better. Try not to put too many expectations on yourself. Being a mother is not like passing a test."

Lydia wiped her eyes. "I feel like I've failed at everything. I'd like to believe what you said, but I just don't. Not the way I feel. I'm in a deep hole. I know you're trying to help. I'm sorry." She began to cry again.

Eric said, "One of the best medicines is time. I want to tell you that you will feel better. It takes time. I know you're working really hard. Try to be gentle with yourself."

"But I haven't got any time." She looked directly at Eric. "The visit is at 1 o'clock this afternoon."

"If you want me to," Dottie offered, "I'll be in the room when you visit with your mom and baby. You don't have to do it all by yourself. Whatever help you need, I'll do it. I'll even change your baby for you."

Lydia smiled for the first time. "Thanks. I'm sorry for taking so much of the group's time. I just don't know what I'll do. There's a nurse who's kind of friendly, maybe she could be with me when my baby comes. I'm so scared that I'll just cry the whole time."

"There's nothing wrong with crying," Eric said. "I think you're wise to have a nurse or someone from the staff to be with you. If it gets too much, they can help you to end the visit. You don't have to face it alone. Maybe as soon as the group is done, you and Dottie can talk. We need to move on now. Is that okay with you?"

Lydia nodded. Eric turned to a good-looking African American guy in a Minnesota Vikings T-shirt. "Hank, you asked for time. Would you like to speak now?"

"Sure. I was admitted last night with a blood alcohol of 0.24. I passed out in the hospital waiting room. When I woke up, I needed to get help. That's why I'm here. Once I'm stable, I'm going into treatment. I need to get off the streets. Alcohol is everywhere. It's in your face out there. If I don't smoke cigarettes, I tip the bottle. If I don't tip the bottle, I take the E." He went on to say how he had lost his girlfriend and his job because of his drinking.

Eric asked, "Has anybody here been in treatment?"

Several patients raised their hands; Jack was one of them. He said, "It's hard, brother. It's all about the aftercare. Most people need to hit rock bottom. Maybe you're there now. This Wednesday at 7:00 p.m. I'll have been sober for nine months." He glanced at Eric. "You can put that in your notes."

Eric smiled, "How's it been for you so far, Hank?"

"This morning I had bad shakes, but they gave me something and now I'm okay. I might have to jump out of group if they come back. I want to change, man. I got the message this time."

Several other group members offered their support to Hank. Eric told him, "Change is hard. They say in AA that everything you let go of has scratch marks on it. It's up to you. But what's happened could be the start of a new life for you, Hank."

"I hope so. The life I had wasn't going anywhere except the gutter. I just need to get through the next few days."

Eric moved us on to Rachel, the final person to ask for time. She was young, pale, and thin. She had about a dozen earrings in one ear and scars up and down both arms. She was a cutter, a self-mutilator.

"I don't need much time today. I'm being discharged this afternoon. I'm bipolar. In a way I like being manic. I could stay up most of the night doing homework and still make it to class. I like to write, and I would sit in a coffee shop with my laptop and write nonstop for hours. OK, maybe I couldn't make sense of it afterwards, but, wow, did I have energy. But it really wasn't so great. I couldn't get to sleep and stopped eating meals. My roommate started to worry about me and called my parents, and they brought me here. I know I sound like a drama queen. But the five days I've been here have been the most important in my life. I've learned so much."

Rachel stopped and smiled. "Excuse me. Sometimes I talk real fast. I have learned that I don't have to be hyperproductive for people to like me. I can slow down. I am a lot better now, but still I have a lot of work to do. I'm afraid of what could happen when I get discharged, that I won't be able to cope. I want to thank Eric and everybody, especially Dottie, who has been here longer than me. My psychiatrist is still working on my dosage of Depakote, but I think that I am on the right track."

"You've helped me too," Dottie told her. "When you first came, I hated you because you were so cute. Now I know that you have problems just like me."

Several group members said goodbye to Rachel and wished her well. Eric told us that we were out of time and that he thought group had gone well.

I had lunch with Dottie, Anna, and Mike, a new patient who was a lawyer. The California burger, fries, and brownie all tasted pretty good— especially the fries, since they, like bacon, were a forbidden food at our house. Just for a moment I paused before eating, a reflex pause to see if I should say grace. Though it is not my habit to say grace in public, I always check when I'm eating in a restaurant with a parishioner to make sure they're not expecting me to say a blessing.

After lunch I read *Fluke* for a while and then went to a recreation group held in a room with a minikitchen along one wall and an upright piano along another. We had the same office chairs there as had been in the therapy room. The group facilitator, a pleasant middle-aged woman, asked us to push our chairs up against the wall to maximize the open space in the center of the room.

She taught us a game, a variation of charades, in which one person had to act out a word in a particular context, after which the rest of the group tried to guess the word. When my turn came, I got the word *frantically*, which I was supposed to act out in the context of a fashion model frantically performing on a runway. Maybe they give *frantically* to all the messed-up ministers who come their way.

I was a smash hit as both an actor and a model. Putting some hip into it, I rapidly sashayed across the room while turning my shirt collar up and down, preening like a possessed fashion model. I pranced, executed an almost-graceful pirouette, and sauntered rapidly around the room again. If you had just come in from the cold and caught my act, you'd have concluded this was the loony bin for sure. But what the hell; I was hot, and I knew it. I could have pranced all night. The group applauded wildly when I was through. I took something between a bow and a curtsy and then twirled back into my chair. The group guessed *embarrassingly, bizarrely, gaily,* and finally *frantically.* I got up and took another bow or curtsy.

As I caught my breath, my frantic modeling career on hold for at least a little while, I thought about how happy I was. What a joy just to do something spontaneously! During all my sashaying and sauntering, I did not think about myself, how absurd I must look, whether I was pleasing the recreation-group leader, or anything else. And I certainly didn't think about my church. I was completely into it, into the moment and outside my own head. What a good time I had!

The day had come full circle from pleasure to all the pain shared in group and then to a wild moment of spontaneous joy. Looking back over the day, I saw how the therapy group and the recreation group, in their different ways, both succeeded in getting me outside my own mind. In the therapy group, the stories and pain of other group members drew me toward them and away from my own concerns. In the recreation group, the role of a frantic model gave me permission to cut loose spontaneously. Sylvia Plath once asked in despair, "Is there no way out of the mind?"[1] In one day, I had found two ways.

The Psalms are a third way. Over time the regular reading of them has worked to free me from my obsessive, self-accusative thoughts. These thoughts were drops of white-hot metal dripping on my naked brain. They were the cause of my head banging, which I had done to make the thoughts stop, or at least to externalize them. The Psalms have proved to be a much less painful and a much more effective way to get these thoughts out of my head. They put the pain into words and bring it to God. They give me some hope that God cares about how much I am hurting and that God might be inclined to do something to heal my hurt.

> Have mercy upon me, O LORD; for I am weak: O LORD, heal me
>   for my bones are vexed.
> My soul is also sore vexed: but thou, O LORD, how long?
> Return, O LORD, deliver my soul: oh save me for thy mercies'
>   sake.
> For in death there is no remembrance of thee: in the grave who
>   shall give thee thanks?
> I am weary with my groaning; all the night make I my bed to
>   swim; I water my couch with my tears. (Psalm 6:2–6)

1. Norris, *Acedia & Me,* 59.

I have groaned until I was weary. I have awakened with my face wet with tears and the rest of me clammy with sweat. My soul has been so sorely vexed that I could not make even the simplest decision. Other psalms that I have cited are equally honest about suffering. Psalm 22 is indeed harrowing in its images of humiliation. But for me Psalm 6 is the most intimate. When I read it, I feel that whoever wrote it knows me personally. I wonder about the author. What exactly happened to him or her to cause such pain? How awful it must have been! While wondering about the author, I'm not obsessing about myself. Psalms like this one are a way out of the mind, both toward God and toward another suffering human being. Consider words from two other laments.

> Save me, O God; for the waters are come in unto my soul.
> I sink in deep mire, where there is no standing: I am come into
>   deep waters, where the floods overflow me.
> I am weary of my crying: my throat is dried: mine eyes fail while
>   I wait for my God. (Psalm 69:1–3)

> For my days are consumed like smoke, and my bones are burned
>   as an hearth.
> My heart is smitten, and withered like grass; so that I forget to
>   eat my bread.
> By reason of the voice of my groaning my bones cleave to my
>   skin.
> I am like a pelican of the wilderness: I am like an owl of the
>   desert.
> I watch, and am as a sparrow alone upon the house top.
>   (Psalm 102:3–7)

I know what it's like to sink into deep mire and to cry out day and night. I know what it's like for my eyes to fail. I know what it's like to forget to eat and then not taste anything when I do eat. And I know what it's like to be so alone in my pain that I feel like a lone sparrow, like a pelican or an owl lost and far from home. The words of those who wrote these psalms thousands of years ago are as true to my experience as the words of Anna, Jack, Dottie, Rachel, and Lydia. Because I know about these friends from the unit, I care about them; I care about those who wrote the laments for the same reason.

In their absolute honesty, the writers of the psalms give hard truth about pain. Their laments are like the huge boulders one sees along the ridge that cuts across southwestern Minnesota. The boulders have been scraped and grooved by the grinding of the glaciers. In a similar way, pain scraped away every defense and evasion of those who wrote the laments, and then they brought their pain to God. Their honesty and courage is a rock-solid foundation for building a relationship with God.

I trust the laments because of their honesty—there's no holding back, no prevaricating, only hard truth. Because these psalms are so honest and true to the pain that I have experienced, I also trust them when they speak of the end of pain, the recovery of pleasure, and the beginning of hope. They lead me from pain and despair to relief and hope. In my recovery and the re-creation of my life of faith, the laments have been the foundation for a renewed relationship to God. I'm still building it, but the foundation is rock solid.

I have learned from studying the Psalms that my experience with the laments is not unique, and that in fact the laments were written in a form that enables this movement toward God. Walter Brueggemann writes about this aspect of the laments in *The Message of the Psalms*:

> The use of these "psalms of darkness" may be judged by the world to be *acts of unfaith and failure*, but for the trusting community, their use is *an act of bold faith*, albeit a transformed faith. It is an act of bold faith on the one hand, because it insists that the world must be experienced as it really is and not in some pretended way. On the other hand, it is bold because it insists that all such experiences of disorder are a proper subject for discourse with God. There is nothing out of bounds, nothing precluded or inappropriate. Everything properly belongs in this conversation of the heart. To withhold parts of life from that conversation is in fact to withhold part of life from the sovereignty of God.[2]

Again from Brueggemann:

> It is no wonder that the church has intuitively avoided these psalms. They lead us into dangerous acknowledgment of how life really is. They lead us into the presence of God where everything is not polite and civil. They cause us to think unthinkable thoughts and utter unutterable words. Perhaps worst, they lead us away from the comfortable religious claims of "modernity" in which everything is managed and controlled . . . The remarkable thing about Israel is that it did not banish or deny the darkness from its religious enterprise. It embraces the darkness as the

---

2. Brueggemann, *Message of the Psalms*, 52.

very stuff of new life. Indeed, Israel seems to know that new life comes nowhere else.[3]

After my hospitalization, after all the pain I have experienced through my own depression, as well as through the stories of my fellow patients, I seek a relationship with God that is the same as what Brueggemann finds in these laments—with no pretending, no denying the way the world really is. It is a relationship where nothing can be held back or declared inappropriate. It is relationship where everything, absolutely everything, can be taken to God in prayer.

If something has to be held back because God can't deal with it, then what's the point? I can do better than that talking to my therapist. But if indeed nothing, however awful, is out of bounds, if nothing needs to be made pretty or polite, if it truly is a relationship based on the way life really is, then I seek it with all my heart. The existence of the laments shows that such a relationship is possible; it's hard to sustain at times, but it is possible.

3. Ibid., 53.

CHAPTER 4

Getting Help with Reality

ON THE UNIT, I lived with people who had been broken by the world and who were no longer able to hide their pain. They were all around me, hunched over their pain, like homeless people over a fire in a garbage can, trying to keep themselves warm late at night. I fit right in.

I know that some of them are still there. I am not. I am one of the lucky ones. I don't mean to be excessively modest. I worked hard at getting well and proved to be good at it. But I also had a lot going for me from the beginning, including money, a house, and a spouse who could make us more money. It is a lot easier to get well when you know your bills are being paid. A lot of people I met on the unit knew for certain that their bills were not being paid. Even more essential to my recovery than money were people who loved me, who wanted to help me, and who could help me. Because of them, I did not get stuck in that place and stay hunched over my pain.

On a psych unit there is no telling what will happen next. It's like a black bear visiting your camp site in the Boundary Waters of northern Minnesota. You're having your morning coffee and watching the mist rise over the lake; you hear something, turn around, and there's the bear. Right after recreation group on my second day on the unit, I got comfortable in the social room with *Fluke* and a cup of a bad coffee (which I was rapidly growing accustomed to). Before I could take a sip, a short white-haired guy in his sixties came up to me and said, "Bob, I'm Dr. Anderson, the psychiatrist who has been assigned to you. How about we go back to your room where we can visit in privacy?"

We walked side by side back to my room, just like two old buddies. With his blue blazer, khakis, blue shirt, and no tie, he could have been a clergy friend or an aging insurance salesman pitching a better policy for my church. What would he charge for rapture insurance? He sat in the chair, and I sat on the side of my unmade bed. To be honest, his opening psychological gambit didn't seem to be all that clever: "So, Bob, what's up?"

What to say to such a probing question? Well, in my case, my need to impress and please those in authority immediately kicked in, and I started telling him how well I was doing. I went on about how much I had learned in group and how much I had learned about myself. What had happened to me, I said, was an aberration. For a brief time all the stars had misaligned, and such a thing would never happen to me again. I felt proud of using an apt and uncommon word like "aberration," and I liked the metaphor of the misaligned stars. As I did so often, I evaluated my talk while I talked.

Dr. Anderson smiled and scratched his head. He needed a haircut. "Swell, Bob. I'm glad things are going so well for you. But I want you to take some time to rest. I've read over what you said at admission, and you've been through a lot. You've been working extremely hard for a long time—too hard. You finally just couldn't do it anymore. And now you're here."

"Well, I feel rested and eager to go home. I think I'm pretty much back to normal now. I just needed a break for a couple of days. I don't think that I need to stay here any longer."

"Bob, slow down. If you had a car with a hundred thousand miles on it and drove it as fast as you could from Minneapolis to Duluth, don't you think you'd begin to smell burnt oil?"

"Yeah, I guess."

"You've been driving yourself too hard and too fast without taking time to recover. Do you know about brain chemistry and neurotransmitters?" I nodded, though I really didn't. "Think of serotonin and norepinephrine as two kinds of oil that you've been burning. You need to take some time to rest and let them build up again. The meds and groups will help, but you need to do your part by learning how not to be so demanding on yourself. You've been burning yourself out. I think it's time for you to slow down."

"Well, I've slowed down a lot since I was admitted."

"How old are you, Bob?"

"Fifty-seven."

He smiled, fingered his coffee cup, and shook his head, "And you've slowed down for less than two days. Bob, from what you told the doctor at admission, I think you push yourself so hard because you interpret things people say to you as nonnegotiable demands, things you can't say no to. I don't know if you do it all the time, but I believe you do it when you are at work. And I believe you do it to yourself by demanding that you meet everybody's expectations. Nobody can do that, and nobody wants you to. You need to be good to yourself for a while. Learn not to interpret what might be a casual suggestion from a person in your church into a demand that you have to meet. Is what I'm saying helpful to you?"

A fragment of a misremembered song came into my head: "I'm just a guy who can't say no." He had me pegged. At church that's all I do every day—try to meet all the demands that people keep hitting me with. That was my life, a litany of demands that not even God Almighty on a good day could meet. So what did this Dr. Anderson want from me?

"Here at the hospital we teach a form of cognitive-behavioral therapy, CBT. It says that just because you think something is true doesn't make it so. Don't believe everything that you think. If you think something is a demand, then you tense up because you think that you have to do what's being demanded. You might also feel resentful about the demand. You get yourself all wrought up about something that isn't really true. People say all sorts of things—make suggestions, think out loud, and tell you their brainstorms. That doesn't mean that they're demanding that you do something."

Had he read the script of my last couple years at church? I had wanted to plead to my parishioners: "Don't you know how hard I am working? Don't you know that I am totally maxed out and have absolutely nothing more to give you people? Why don't you cut me some slack and give me a break? Doesn't anybody around here see that I am doing the best I can? For Christ's sake, help me." Of course I didn't plead, and I didn't ask for help. I just worked harder.

When I started paying attention to him again, Dr. Anderson was in the process of telling me what to do. "One way to work on this is to pay attention in group to what people say that triggers an emotional response in you. If you feel tense, resentful, or anxious, ask yourself what thoughts are causing those feelings. By bringing these thoughts out into the open, you can see if they are rational or not. Whatever you do in group will be okay. I'm just giving you some suggestions that I think will be helpful to you. You know yourself a lot better than I do."

Dr. Anderson took a swig of his coffee and then smiled. Over time I got to know that this is what he always did before telling one of his parables. "You know, Bob, I think you are like a knight who has spent years polishing up his heavy armor until it shines like the sun. Then he goes off to a jousting match. But instead of finding other knights in armor with lances, there are guys with felt hats and machine guns."

He must have seen the look of absolute incomprehension on my face, or maybe he feared I was thinking of throwing popcorn at him. At any rate he was quick with the interpretation: "You see, the defenses and skills that you have learned in order to deal with stress are outdated and don't work for you anymore. Like the knight's armor, they are not adequate to cope with the challenges of your life. CBT and group will help you to see this and to learn more effective ways of coping. You are bright and skilled. This is something that you will be able to work on over time. I have to go now, but I'll be back to visit with you tomorrow."

After he left, I wrote down on the back of a green flyer as much as I could remember of what he had said. In spite of his insights, I was still disappointed in him. I guess I had expected my psychiatrist to look a little less shabby and to come across as a lot more erudite. Then again, I have a poor record of dealing with authority figures. At least Dr. Anderson didn't try to rub his authority in my face.

And I had to admit that what he had said about cognitive-behavioral therapy fit my own behavior. In group the thought that Jack's anger was somehow my responsibility had triggered anxiety and other bad feelings. And at church when somebody said that something needed to be done, I always heard the statement as a demand that I make sure that it did get done. I resented the demand. I bit my tongue—literally, on occasion—but I never objected.

As I reflected on my conversation with Dr. Anderson, I started to tense up. He obviously knew a lot about me, more than he could have learned from reading my admission reports. I suspected that he and Eric were sharing files on what I did and said. I had better be careful. I had learned to be careful around lots of people over my years in ministry: church leaders, denominational executives, anyone I perceived as having power over me. I added Dr. Anderson to the list. Better be careful.

Consistent with what Dr. Anderson had said, we had education groups on the unit where we learned more about the rudiments of CBT. Our group leader suggested that if we wanted to go deeper into CBT, we could buy a copy of *Feeling Good* by David Burns. It's kind of a how-to book for CBT.

Months later, when I felt better and could concentrate, I followed his suggestion. I found particularly helpful the beginning chapters where Burns describes different kinds of "cognitive distortions" that trigger negative thoughts.[1] When brought to mind, such cognitive distortions can be rationally challenged.

Burns calls one particularly common kind of distortion "labeling and mislabeling."[2] For example, I believed that I was a failure in my ministry and felt unbearable pain because of this. But is this thought logical? And is *a failure* an accurate label for me as a minister? In fact, didn't I have many successes: church growth, people genuinely helped, mission projects completed, and so on? In fact, haven't I received a wealth of positive feedback? (*Feedback* is such an inadequate word. Over the years parishioners had hugged me, wept in gratitude, told me that I had saved their lives. This is more than feedback.)

Now back to CBT: isn't it true that nobody succeeds all the time? Even Mark Trail makes mistakes. Making mistakes is part of the reality of being human. Yes, like everybody else, I made some mistakes in my work. But overall, if I had to use a label—and labels are always dangerous—*success* would be a more accurate label than *failure*.

CBT has also helped me to face a common reality of my profession. All preachers know the drill: after church you shake hands with departing parishioners and hear a chorus of "Good job," "Nice sermon," "Thank you," "You always have a good message." (If you don't hear this chorus at least once in a while, then in reality you should attend a refresher class on preaching or find another line of work.) But then toward the end, just when you think you will be able to go home and enjoy the afternoon, somebody comes up, most likely a trustee or a prominent giver, who says something like "Good job, Pastor Bob, but I'd like to ask you more about something you said. Maybe give me a call sometime."

Of all the comments, which one stays with me? The last one, of course. So I start to brood about what might have bothered the trustee. What did I say? How badly did I offend him? Will he withhold his contributions? Will he share his displeasure with other powerful members?

---

1. Burns, *Feeling Good*, 32–43.
2. Ibid., 39.

Can I get a new job real fast? Of course this is rampant overgeneraliza-
tion, but it's what happens.

And what do I do about all the positive comments? Don't they
count for anything? Not for me. According to this negative thought pat-
tern, these parishioners said positive things just to be nice. After all, my
church members are Minnesotans. Nice is what we do. So I brood all
afternoon and then have trouble getting to sleep. The next morning, after
a miserable night, I dredge up the courage to call the trustee to find out
what he wants to talk about. Will he tell me that he wants my immediate
resignation?

"Oh yeah, Pastor. Thanks for calling. Isn't this supposed to be your
day off, by the way? At any rate, you said something about the Social Gospel in your sermon yesterday. That sounds interesting and maybe there's
something I can learn from it about how to be a better Christian through
my work. Do you have a book on the history of the Social-Gospel movement that I could borrow? By the way, did you see the Twins yesterday
afternoon? What a great game! If the starters keep pitching the way they
have been these last few weeks, we have a real shot to make the playoffs.
You know what? My company has season tickets right behind home plate.
Would you like a pair?"

In CBT terms, my cognitive distortions include "jumping to conclu-
sions" (which is pretty obvious) and "all-or-nothing thinking," moving
quickly from one possibly negative comment to the possibility of losing
my job. Burns writes, "All-or-nothing thinking forms the basis for per-
fectionism. It causes you to fear any mistake or imperfection because you
will then see yourself as a complete loser, and you will feel inadequate and
worthless."[3] Like the authors of the laments, Dr. Burns knows me well.

My thinking also includes a kind of cognitive distortion Burns calls
"mental filter." This happens when you "pick out a negative detail in any
situation and dwell on it exclusively, thus perceiving the whole situation
is negative."[4] Finally it includes "disqualifying the positive," failing to let
all the positive feedback count for anything.[5] When you become aware of
just how distorting all these cognitive distortions can be, it's almost funny, except that the feelings that these distortions cause can distort your

3. Ibid., 32.
4. Ibid., 34.
5. Ibid., 34–36.

relationships, cripple you as a professional, leech away all your pleasures, and leave you banging your head against a wall.

In his work with me, Dr. Anderson used CBT in the same way that he used his stories: as a way to get me out of my head and into the real world where cognitive distortions can be seen for what they are. On his next visit with me he retold me the story about the knight polishing his armor and how I needed to learn new ways of coping. In this way, Anderson reminded me of a preacher who loved to repeat his favorite sermon illustration, sometimes forgetting that he used it the previous Sunday.

He went on to say that learning new ways of coping isn't easy.

"Bob, there are times when we need to take a risk and behave differently. When you go back to work, it's important that you use what you've learned here. If you try to do the same things the same way you have in the past, you won't get better. Changing old behaviors is difficult, but it's necessary, and finally the risk is worth it. You've been taking that risk here, and I believe that you have made a lot of progress. I just want you to keep it up."

"I'd like for you to spend some time just thinking about how you could do things differently in your life and work. For example, you'll need to be able to say no, take time for yourself away from work, and let your parishioners know that you're doing it. You know, I believe that if you told your parishioners 'I'll do this, but I won't do that,' they'd treat you like you were able to walk on water."

I said from my heart, "Dr. Anderson, the people in my church would do anything for me. They'll let me make the changes that I need to make."

"You're fortunate. And I suspect the people in the church are this way because you have been a caring pastor for so long. They have learned from you. It's good that they will look after you. But you need to look after yourself too. You know an old rubber band doesn't snap back as fast as a new one. You'll need to give yourself some time to snap back before you go back to work. And once you get back, it will be important not to try to do more than you can. Imagine one of your church members looking at you and saying, 'There's old Bob. Doesn't he look funny trying to carry the whole church around on his back?' I'm concerned that if you go back too soon, you'll try to do too much. Let other people help you in your work." He smiled. "I've learned to let other people do as much work for me as they want to."

So, he's lazy. I knew it! Finally I mustered the courage to ask him point-blank when I could be discharged. This directness was new behavior for me. I was moving along.

"Christmas," he said.

"Christmas?"

"It's OK, Bob. Don't take everything I say so seriously. Besides, with me any day can be Christmas. And why are you in such a hurry to leave this nice warm hospital when it's still freezing outside? We'll talk about your discharge more tomorrow. See you then."

"Fine. But you know that for me tomorrow will be Christmas."

"Could be, Bob. Could be."

Dr. Anderson's stories about cars burning oil, knights polishing armor, and old rubber bands made me feel tired and old—probably not what he intended. They also helped me to see that I had more work to do in my recovery than I could ever do on my own, which is probably what he intended. I needed people to help me rest, to help carry the burdens of my life, to point me in the right direction, and then to walk with me that way for a while.

Like bears in the woods, help abounded in the hospital: Dr. Anderson, Eric, my groups, and my friends on my unit. Once I walked out of the hospital doors, my family, friends, colleagues, and parishioners would be there for me. Of course, in the hospital you didn't really have to ask for help. It's what the staff did for a living. But to get help outside the hospital—except from Sue, my children, and our best friends—I would have to learn how to ask for help.

I suspect that it's the pride I learned from my dad that made me averse to asking for help, though of course doing it on your own is part of the American-male ethos. John Wayne didn't go around begging for help. Of course he was quite good with a rifle. Well, I'm not John Wayne, and I'm unarmed. By failing to ask for help, I caused much avoidable pain to myself and others. I will always grieve this. I served a church that was full of good people eager to help me, people who needed to help me, and I didn't ask.

Of course, to let people help me, I needed also to trust them. My church was full of good people, but in reality there were also a few terribly needy folks that could not help me and would make things worse, and there were one or two who did not have helping me or anyone else on their life agenda. I guess out in the world, even the church world, you do need to know whom to ask for help.

Given my ambivalence toward authority and my suspicion about the staff's plans for me, it took a while for me to trust Dr. Anderson and Eric. But I did learn to trust them. Indeed, I suspect that much of their success as professionals comes from how they get suspicious people like me to trust them. Then again, there are people like Jack, who had a lot more reason to be suspicious than I did. I'm not sure that Jack ever did build up trust. I'm not sure that he ever got well either.

As I learned to receive help, I became like one of the runners in the book of Hebrews.

> Wherefore seeing we also are compassed about with so great a cloud of witnesses, let us lay aside every weight, and the sin which doth so easily beset us, and let us run with patience the race that is set before us. (Heb 12:1)

That's what I want to do: run the race of recovery with patience while letting others encourage and sustain me. It's a very long race; I need to pace myself, as Dr. Anderson cautioned. At times I'm tempted to quit and just lie in bed with a pillow over my face, but I have so many people cheering me on. I can't let them and myself down. And there are people who ran the race before me, like those who wrote the psalms of lament. I owe them my best effort. When I look around, I also see that there are lots of people running with me now. At the moment I'm running with Anna, Dottie, Lydia, Rachel, Hank, and even Jack. With such a crowd, the race can even be fun. There are lots of people to swap stories with.

In the book of Hebrews the things that weigh us down in our race are called sins. Dr. Anderson called them old ways of coping that don't work anymore. In CBT they are called ways of illogical thinking. I have described several of these and have explained how they weigh me down. There is yet one more, the heaviest of all. Burns calls it "personalization." He writes, "This distortion is the mother of guilt! You assume responsibility for the negative even when there is no basis for doing so. You arbitrarily conclude that what happened was your fault or reflects your inadequacy, even when you were not responsible for it."[6]

A little later Burns writes, "Personalization causes you to feel crippling guilt. You suffer from a paralyzing and burdensome sense of responsibility that forces you to carry the whole world on your shoulders."[7]

6. Ibid., 40.
7. Ibid., 41.

If I am going to run the race, I have to get the weight of personalization off my back.

I personalize when I blame myself for what is not my responsibility, not only blaming myself for conflict among church members, but also for most everything else. In my work, I had come to take responsibility for any bad outcome, no matter how much it was out of my control or beyond the parameters of my job description. This ended in disaster. In trying to do everybody else's job at church, I became too exhausted to do my own job.

Parker Palmer, who is also a recovering depressive, calls the theology underlying personalization "functional atheism," which is "the belief that ultimate responsibility for everything rests with us."[8] The functional atheists say all kinds of pious things about God but in reality don't trust God or anybody else. They have deposed God in favor of themselves. They, not God, will get 'er done (to use a phrase that is loved in western Minnesota). Theologically this is not only functional atheism; it is also a violation of the first commandment, which implies that God alone is the one who gets 'er done.

In the last couple years, I had become a functional atheist in my ministry, a solo act running the "church of Bob." As Dr. Anderson said, I had put the church on my back, asking neither God nor anybody else to give me a hand. By doing other people's jobs for them, I had deprived members of their own opportunities to serve God through serving their church, so worsening the quality of my own ministry. It's all so sad, so arrogant, and so destructive. I acted as if the church was at my disposal. I had forgotten that in the United Church of Christ, Jesus Christ, not Bob, is the head of the church.

As I have learned not to personalize, I have become a much better minister. I don't have to do everything, and I can let others take responsibility and leadership. This includes responsibility for the pastoral care of other members. I have learned the hard way about helping, and allowing oneself to be helped. I have a passion for this work that others catch from me. I think that I caught it from my mom.

In a congregation where I recently served in an interim position, we called this reciprocal helping ministry congregational care. Helping is what the congregation does. It is not just the prerogative of the pastor. Together, as Galatians 6:2 says, we "bear one another's burdens" and so

8. Palmer, *Let Your Life Speak*, 88.

"fulfill the law of Christ" (NRSV). With congregational care, we greatly extended our ability to do this: obviously several people can give more help than one person can. It's really that simple. How I now engage my church in the ministry of helping leads to a wonderful paradox: doing less myself as pastor, I accomplish more as pastor.

In another type of congregational care, I often preach on psalms like Psalm 104, which offer a vision of the good life to be found when you venture outside yourself. These psalms open your eyes to the fullness of reality's banquet and even pull up a chair for you at the table. Here are words from Psalm 104:

> The trees of the LORD are full of sap; the cedars of Lebanon,
>   which he hath planted;
> Where the birds make their nests: as for the stork, the fir trees
>   are her house.
> The high hills are a refuge for the wild goats: and the rocks for
>   the conies.
> He appointed the moon for seasons: the sun knoweth his going
>   down.
> Thou makest darkness, and it is night: wherein all the beasts of
>   the forest do creep forth.
> The young lions roar after their prey, and seek their meat from
>   God.
> The sun ariseth, they gather themselves together, and lay them
>   down in their dens. (Psalm 104:16–22)

These images delight our senses and draw us into the world. They overwhelm our tendencies to personalize and to take responsibility for that which is so obviously and totally beyond our control. The moon and the sun don't need us. The storks, goats, conies, and especially the lions aren't counting on us. There is nothing for us to do except be still and let all that is life draw us toward it and away from our preoccupation with ourselves.

For me the celebration of reality's richness in the Bible climaxes with the book of Job. The book is about many things, including how to help and how not to. Job's friends, his famous "comforters," come and sit with him in silence for a symbolic seven days and seven nights, simply letting him know that he is not alone. This is how to help when words fail. But when they do start talking, they show that they should have kept silent. Maybe they should have given Job a group foot rub and then gone on their way. By the pious things they say (words for their own comfort and not for Job's), they show how one can turn helping into hurting. When words fail, we must keep silent.

At the end of the book of Job comes another attempt to help, one that I believe is successful in moving Job beyond his own concerns, as legitimate as they are, and back into reality. Job has sought to question God about human concerns: Why do the innocent suffer? Specifically, why am I, an innocent man, in agony right now? Instead of answering Job's questions, God turns the tables and questions him about God's concerns. This is God's first step in getting Job to think about someone besides himself.

Job wants justice; God gives him reality as seen through the eyes of his Creator. God gives it to him in a series of images so startling that Job is overwhelmed. God shows him that much of reality is beyond human understanding, and that God's ways are not our ways. Job is in no position to judge. However, he is, by the grace of God, a part of this reality, and he can share in its abundance. God takes Job's hand and puts his fingers on the pulse of so much life.

> Gavest thou the goodly wings unto the peacocks? or wings and feathers unto the ostrich?
> Which leaveth her eggs in the earth, and warmest them in dust,
> And forgetteth that the foot may crush them, or that the wild beast may break them.
> She is hardened against her young ones, as though they were not hers: her labor is in vain without fear;
> Because God hath deprived her of wisdom, neither hath he imparted to her understanding. What time she lifteth up herself on high, she scorneth the horse and his rider.
> Hast thou given the horse strength? hast thou clothed his neck with thunder?
> Canst thou make him afraid as a grasshopper? the glory of his nostrils is terrible.
> He paweth in the valley, and rejoiceth in his strength, he goeth on to meet the armed men.
> He mocketh at fear, and is not affrighted; neither turneth he back from the sword.
> The quiver rattleth against him, the glittering spear and the shield.
> He swalloweth the ground with fierceness and rage: neither believeth he that it is the sound of the trumpet.
> He saith among the trumpets, Ha, ha; and he smelleth the battle afar off, the thunder of the captains, and shouting.

> Doth the hawk fly by thy wisdom, and stretch her wings toward
>   the south?
> Doth the eagle mount up at thy command, and make her nest
>   on high?
> She dwelleth and abideth on the rock, upon the crag of the rock,
>   and the strong place.
> From thence she seeketh the prey, and her eyes behold afar off.
> Her young ones also suck up blood: and where the slain are,
>   there is she. (Job 39:13–30)

We would have to be as forgetful as the ostrich and as heedless of the reality around us to imagine that this vast carnival is about us. It's about God's prodigality with the gift of life, evolving in highways and byways beyond one's imagining. We are part of a whole that we understand no better than a grasshopper understands the mighty horse. Read this passage again; savor all the reality that it evokes. By God's grace, you may be moved to the only rational act one can perform in response to the ostrich, horse, hawk, and eagle: to offer up a doxology, to praise God from whom all this life flows.

And while you offer up the doxology, also thank God because God seeks to engage us as God engaged Job. We do not take the journey into reality alone. God is with us in our journey through the valley of the shadow of death, and God hosts the potluck afterwards. Job's comforters tried so hard to help, but they just could not keep their mouths shut. God knows exactly how to help—more often by showing than by telling. Granted, you have to go out a bit on the limb of faith to believe all this, but I encourage you, and myself, to keep working on it.

These chapters from the book of Job have helped heal me from my major depression and anxiety disorder. Three times in *The Jesuit Guide to (Almost) Everything: A Spirituality for Real Life*, James Martin, SJ, quotes Walter Burghardt's definition of prayer as a "long, loving look at the real."[9] By this definition, what I have written in this chapter is a prayer of gratitude. I have learned from "whence cometh my help" (Psalm 121:1).

I'll close with a reality story of my own. I was serving as a supply pastor in a medium-sized church in a university town. In classic congregational architectural style, the church has its communion table on pew level, right in front of the central pulpit that stands on a raised platform. Jonathan Edwards would have been perfectly at home. Though, come to

9. Martin, *Jesuit Guide*, 8.

think of it, he might have raised an eyebrow at the large candle on the table: a little too popish for his taste.

Since the pulpit is raised and removed from the congregation, I spoke most of the liturgy in front of the communion table so that I could be closer to the people. I used the pulpit for some of my sermons. One Sunday a member approached me and said that she was worried about my doing so much of the liturgy and the prayers in front of the communion table. I explained to her that I wanted to be close to the congregation during worship. I went on to tell her that God was present in the congregation so that when I prayed facing the congregation, I was speaking to God's spirit in their midst. In short, I opened up a can of theology on her.

She listened to me with patience and good humor. When I was finally done with my lecture, she said, "Pastor, that's all very nice and as far as I'm concerned, you can pray wherever you want to pray. But you see, while you're in front of that table talking and praying, you keep leaning backwards and getting closer to the candle. I'm afraid you're going to catch yourself on fire."

That's exactly the help I need in facing reality.

CHAPTER 5

Recovering Self-Respect

I AM LEARNING TO love reality, but as I wrote earlier, what we folks in the United Church of Christ really love are paradoxes. If you are like us, then you will love this chapter. It is all about a paradox. Even better, the paradox is more existential than logical, so you get to live it. The place where I landed after my freedom had been taken away and after I had proved a failure in managing my own life turned out to be the place where I also starting getting back my self-respect. How is that for a paradox?

By my third day on the unit, I had settled into a routine: breakfast, followed by group, then lunch, another group after lunch, followed by some kind of recreational activity and time to hang out, and finally supper, followed by a TV movie before bedtime. A few days earlier, going to work and church meetings had defined my schedule. Yet I adapted quickly to my new life, to both its routines and its peculiar moments, as when a nurse pops into your room to ask if we are feeling suicidal this morning.

By my third CMP group session, Rachel had been discharged and Hank had been referred to a chemical-dependency group. There were two new patients in my group, Norman and Jane. At goal setting, Norman told us that he was a professor of English at the University of Minnesota. I recognized him from the night before, when he had arrived on my unit. A large man with a barrel chest and impressive tufts of chest hair showing above the V in his pajama tops, he looked more like a professional wrestler gone to seed than a professor.

Jane was an attractive woman in her late teens. She sat with her arms folded tightly across her chest. She wore a long-sleeved men's white shirt. From my experience with Rachel, I was pretty sure that I knew what the long sleeves meant. She said, "My goal for today is to not commit suicide. I want to hurt myself, but not bad enough to die. My parents committed me because I cut myself too deep."

Eric said, "Jane, I respect your honesty. I need to be honest also and say that if you try to harm yourself while you're here, we're required to put you on Dangerous Behavior Protocol. You'll be watched carefully and won't be able to come to group."

"I'm not going to hurt myself here. That's not what I mean. I'm back on my meds and they're uppers. Not that I feel like dancing. I just don't see that anything in my life has really changed or is going to change while I'm in here."

"Okay," Eric said, "I accept where you are right now. Let's start there."

Dottie, Lydia, and I asked for time. I had not asked for time the previous group, and I needed at least some class-participation credit. This isn't being totally honest or fair to myself. I also wanted and needed the group's support.

Lydia said that she would go first. She was wearing the same T-shirt with a white kitten on it that she had worn two days ago, only since then she had spilled coffee on the bottom of it. "I was too sick to come to group yesterday. But just to let you know, I did visit with my baby on Thursday. He's the reason that I'm here." She looked down and picked up her wad of tissue.

"That's not fair. I don't know why I said that. It's not him, but I got the depression after he was born. The visit went pretty good. I was real scared at first—like if I touched him, he would start crying. But it turned out that I was able to hold him almost the whole time. A nurse or some-body was there at the beginning, but she left once she saw that I was okay. My mom was good too. She got it. She said she would take some time from work after I get discharged to be at home with me and the baby. I'm going to talk to my psychiatrist about being discharged."

"What was the difference between seeing your baby here and being with your baby before you were hospitalized?" Eric asked.

"Most of all, I knew that I had help. I wasn't so afraid of what I would do if the baby started to cry."

Eric said, "Babies need to cry. It's their job. It's not your fault. Your baby is just doing what he needs to do."

"I guess. I had an idea of the kind of mother I'd be, and I can't do it. God knows how much I want to. You know, last night I remembered that I hadn't even told you my baby's name. It's Michael Joseph."

"That's a good name," Dottie said. "And you're a good mother. Just know that whatever happens, we'll be cheering for you."

"Thanks. I know that."

I went after Lydia. I told the group that for weeks before I was hospitalized, I tried to act normal at my church while there was a roaring in my ears and my stomach felt clenched. "All this time, I felt like the worst kind of phony. I wasn't connected to what I was saying. It was like somebody else was talking. I was a zombie. Mostly I was playing for time, hoping to keep people happy with me and hoping that I'd wake up one morning and be all better. Maybe God would have given me a great big hug while I slept or at least given me a good night's sleep. But it never happened. I kept waking up feeling worse than when I had gone to bed. So finally I had a meltdown, and now I'm here."

"Do you feel like a phony now?" Eric asked.

"Not right now. I'm trying to be completely honest. What have I got to lose? Are they going to come and lock me up? It's a huge relief not to have to put on an act anymore."

"I feel like you are telling the truth," Norman said. "I know what it feels like to be a hypocrite. I'm a teacher, but I've been just going through the motions. I can't concentrate on my work or my students. They call me 'professor,' 'doctor,' and 'sir.' I want to laugh. I'm a joke."

Dottie spoke up, "Bob, you don't sound like a phony to me. You don't when we eat together, and you don't here in group." She leaned forward and stared into my face, "And I can smell a phony a mile away."

I thanked both of them and said that I was worried about the backlash. "What would people think of me when they realized that I had been putting on an act for so long? How could they trust me or think that I would do them any good?"

"I'm not sure you heard what Dottie said," Eric responded. "She said you don't come across as a phony now. You're not putting on an act for us. How does it feel just to be who you are?"

"It feels good. I feel like I can breathe now. At church I never feel like I can just relax and take a deep breath. If I say the wrong thing, somebody will quit, and I'll get blamed for it. I'm always on call, always in the role of pastor, and never free just to say what I think. At the same time, I'm supposed to be honest in my preaching, like a prophet telling truth that the people don't want to hear. What a phony and a hypocrite I am!"

While Eric was answering me, I bit down hard on the inside of my cheek, my first self-punitive act since being admitted.

When I came back to the present, Eric was talking to me. I had no idea how long I had been lost in my head. He said that trying to be who we aren't is trying to lead a fraudulent life. At least that is what I think he was saying. He said that doing this is painful and stressful. The hospital is a safe place to think about what we really want in our lives. We need to live lives that are true to who we are if we are going to be happy. I thanked him and the group. I told them that I needed some time to let what they had said sink in.

Dottie spoke after me. "I'd like to say I'm feeling better, that things are going good—but they aren't. When I think about my insurance company and all the hassles I have getting it to pay for my treatment, I get really pissed off. And I'm angry at my boyfriend for being such a jerk-off. I'm angry at the mechanic who said he'd fix my car free if I fucked him. I'm so angry right now that I could get up and pound these walls. Look, I'm not going to do it, but that's how I feel."

Eric asked, "Dottie, what do you gain by getting so angry?"

"Gain?" Dottie thought a minute, tracing the unicorn tattooed on her arm. "When I'm pissed off, I feel like I want to slug somebody, but I don't think that I'm gaining anything. Sometimes when I get angry at work, I come home and clean the house. Maybe that's something I get out of it."

"I know how that feels," Jack said. He had been quiet until then, seemingly not paying any attention. "When I get mad, I get rid of it by working out. I'm trying my best not to be angry being here. I'd rather be in jail. At least when you are in jail, you know where you stand. They leave you alone. Here I feel like someone wants to document every breath."

Eric said, "Dottie, you have every right to be angry about how you've been treated, but you can't be angry all the time. You'll wear yourself out. Do you think that you deserve to be happy and to be in a good relationship?"

"Nobody ever asked me that before. Nobody ever tried to make me happy." Her eyes glistened. "I don't think anybody out there gives a damn."

"We do in here," Lydia said. "You were a real help to me yesterday. You're a very sincere person. Everything you say is from the heart. I want you to be happy."

Several other group members joined in support of Dottie. I told her how much I admired her strength and courage. I didn't tell her that compared to her, I felt like I had an easy life with no real reason to complain about anything. Reality had kicked her in the gut, while I was just kicking myself. When it came to blessings, I had so many, starting with Sue and the boys. She didn't have much of anything. I had a soft life, but I still messed it up. What an asshole I am!

Eric told Dottie, "Dottie, people here have said that they care about you. You do deserve to be happy and to have good relationships. A lot of crappy things have happened to you, but you have kept on fighting back. I have a lot of respect for you."

"I don't have a lot of choice about fighting back, do I? I can't stay here forever, not with what this hospital costs. I'm sorry. I know I come across angrier than I am. Sometimes I feel like it's either fight or go down the sewer. I'm tired, really beat. That's all I want to say today. I'm going to shut up now."

"This is a safe place to be tired and to rest," Eric said. "Just know that you are a respected member of this group." Dottie looked at him and nodded her head.

Eric went on to draw the group to a close: "One thing we learn in group is how other people see us. With depression and bipolar disorder, our self-image becomes distorted. We need other people to help us see ourselves as we really are. I think the group has done that for those who spoke today. Remember that tomorrow is Sunday, so we won't have group."

I went into my room to scribble notes and to think over what had happened in group. The inside of my cheek was really tender and bleeding a little bit, but my urge to hurt myself had died down. Thinking about Dottie and all that she had been through had gotten me out of my self-absorption and self-disgust.

Still doing the homework that Dr. Anderson had requested, I looked for the triggering thought. Why had I had felt as I did in group, and why had I wanted to hurt myself? This was easy: once I had labeled myself as a phony, my self-hatred had taken over. I intentionally bit myself for being a phony just when I was being as honest as I could be with the group. I just won't give myself a break.

In our different ways, all of us in group were struggling to regain our self-respect. It seemed that Dottie had been disrespected by everyone who crossed her path—except for those of us in group. Lydia could not be the mother she imagined, and this was eating away at her self-confidence and self-respect. Norman struggled to respect himself as a teacher, and I struggled to respect myself as a minister. In ways very different from the rest of us, Jack fought for self-respect, as well as for the respect, even the fear, of other people.

Given what I have learned from people in the hospital, I know that without recovering self-respect one cannot recover mental health. In "On Self-Respect," an essay collected in *Slouching towards Bethlehem*, Joan Didion writes: "To have that sense of one's intrinsic worth which constitutes self-respect is potentially to have everything: the ability to discriminate, to love and to remain indifferent."[1]

She also tells what it costs not to have self-respect: "To do without self-respect, on the other hand, is to be an unwilling audience of one to an interminable documentary that details one's failings, both real and imagined, with fresh footage spliced in for every screening."[2]

This is so true to my own experience of depression that I wonder if maybe in some past life, like the authors of the lament, Didion knew me personally. I think that self-respect is like generosity, gratitude, honesty, and courage. It is one of the virtues determining how you live your life. If you work at it, you can get better at it, just as practice improves playing the piano, ice-skating, or preaching. All the virtues are like this. To learn the virtue of gratitude, you have to act like a grateful person: you take the time to say a complete thank-you, and you take the time to write those detailed thank-you notes. Likewise, if you want to be a generous person, you have to practice generosity. If every time there is an opportunity to give, you keep your wallet closed or your purse snapped shut, you will never become generous, will you?

The same is true of the virtue of self-respect. How can you say that you have self-respect if you kick yourself around and allow others to do the same?

These virtues aren't merely mental. They are something that you practice in the real world. If you fail, that's sad but acceptable as long as, following the counsel of Ms. Didion, you take responsibility for your failure.

The virtue of self-respect includes admitting your mistakes and accepting responsibility, but it excludes reflexively blaming yourself for everything that goes wrong. A person with self-respect takes appropriate responsibility and stops right there. Self-respect includes lamenting life's tragic losses, but it excludes whining over life's inconveniences and

1. Didion, *Slouching towards Bethlehem*, 147.
2. Ibid., 143–44.

routine disappointments. Self-respect is tough and honest, like a friend who cares enough about you to tell you the truth.

One sees here a balancing and a maintenance of proportion in the practice of self-respect: yes but also no. Take responsibility for this, but not for that. Losing my own sense of proportion, failing to keep responsibilities in realistic balance, I lost my self-worth and my self-respect, and I fell into depression. It destroyed my life as I knew it. As Amma Syncletica, a fourth-century desert nun, wrote, "Lack of proportion always corrupts."[3]

Underlying this desert mother's words is a deep understanding of the roots of human nature that ground self-respect in self-worth. There is a kind of ultimate balance that defines who we are. You can find it in the words from Psalm 8, which I quote from the New Revised Standard Version:

> When I look at your heavens, the work of your fingers, the moon
>   and the stars that you have established;
> what are human beings that you are mindful of them, mortals
>   that you care for them?
> Yet you have made them a little lower than God, and crowned
>   them with glory and honor. (Psalm 8:3–5)

In this psalm our self-worth, and hence our self-respect, is grounded in God, who is our maker. When I was a youth pastor, back in the Nixon and Ford administrations, we used to give the kids T-shirts with the slogan "God doesn't make junk." (Given how many of our youth today are bullied and attempt suicide, maybe it's time to make some more of these T-shirts.) In a nutshell, "God doesn't make junk" is what these verses from Psalm 8 are telling us. Since God made us and crowned us with glory and honor, who are we to disrespect ourselves or allow others to disrespect us?

For Christians, of course, this assertion of human self-worth fulfills itself in the life, death, and resurrection of Jesus Christ, the very Son of God given for us. This is what Paul writes to the Corinthians: "For I delivered unto you first of all that which I also received, how that Christ died for our sins according to the scriptures" (1 Corinthians 15:3). The logic is inevitable: if God loved us enough to make such a sacrifice for our sake, shouldn't we also love ourselves? "Smile; God loves you" is a slogan

3. Norris, *Dakota*, 213.

that I don't like as much as "God doesn't make junk," but it also makes the point.

For people of faith, intrinsic self-worth is thus grounded in the love of God. However, this does not mean that we are God, as a functional atheist tries to be. If we are to avoid corruption, there is a balance to be maintained here. Psalm 8 reminds us that though our birthright is lofty, we are born mortals. As mortals, we get things wrong from time to time—sometimes quite frequently.

In his letter to the Romans, Paul writes, "For all have sinned, and come short of the glory of God" (Romans 3:23). Later in Romans, he reveals his own struggle with sin: "For that which I do, I allow not: for what I would, that do I not; but what I hate, that do I" (Romans 7:15) and "For the good that I would I do not: but the evil which I would not, that I do" (Romans 7:19).

Self-respect keeps who we are as God's beloved children in balance with what we sometimes do: we are God's beloved children who sin. And lest you think all this talk of sin is too "old school," remember that it is simply a theological way of saying that we are not perfect and never will be. It's a liberating admission of reality, which is, of course, essential for self-respect.

Like the writers of the laments, Paul doesn't pretend. He tells us who we really are. As a minster, I feel the temptation, which Brueggemann cites, to be relentlessly positive, to avoid hard realities, certainly to avoid talking about something as downbeat as sin. Of course it's a good thing to be positive when you can, but not at the cost of being real. It's good to preach on the joy that comes in the morning. But who will believe you if you ignore the weeping that endures for the night? Besides, whatever you say, your congregation can tell when you're denying the way things really are.

Just as we constantly need to hear the message of our intrinsic self-worth, we need to hear the message of the sins that cling to us. Otherwise we will lose our sense of proportion. Without this, we will constantly be tripping over our own limits by pursuing perfection, which is not possible for us. To keep moving ahead in the race, we must claim both of these realities. So doing, we are neither puffed up nor deflated, but we have just the right amount of air to breathe easily.

Through living with depression, I have come to this understanding of sin as a lack of proportion. I am not saying that I understand the depths of sin as a theological topic, only that this is how, following Paul and others, I experience it. According to Richard Crouter in *Reinhold Niebuhr: On Politics, Religion, and Christian Faith*, this is much the same understanding of sin that Reinhold Niebuhr came to through his "Christian realist" analysis of human nature.

> We need to remind ourselves of Niebuhr's complexity of mind, especially the fact that self-preoccupation makes us poor judges in our own cases. We are not evil so much as warped by pride or sloth that arises from the lack of equilibrium between mind, body, and will. As creatures we are in the natural order with our wants and desires; yet our human glory and that of science lie in our capacity to stand above ourselves to make new discoveries and to weigh moral choices, including the fate of the earth.[4]

As a person who fell into the pit of depression, unable to do anything, I have veered between the heights of pride as a "functional atheist" and the depths of sloth. Recovering my self-respect, I have found the balance between the two, my own "golden mean" (to draw Aristotle into the discussion). As a Christian I understand this recovery as forgiveness, my restoration to fullness of life through the grace of God in Christ. It's wonderful to discover my kinship not only with the desert Amma but also with Niebuhr and Aristotle. It does a lot for my self-respect.

When too many things come at me and I am in danger of losing proportion or equilibrium, I have help close at hand. The psalms and other Scriptures help keep my life in balance. So does careful attending to the words of those who are trying to help us by holding up a mirror to our behavior. This is what I so often experienced in group. A good therapist like Dr. Anderson is also adept at helping us reclaim our self-worth while accepting our limitations. An honest preacher can do the same.

For me, humor is another way that I have kept my balance in the world. It has been important for me that I wrote my doctor of ministry dissertation on humor in pastoral care. I described how humor is connected with humus (the earth) and with being human (the people of the earth). Seeing the humor in our pretensions—laughing gently at ourselves—keeps us grounded. It keeps us down-to-earth and close to the real. When we, especially we clergy, get too far off the ground, too pretentious and perfectionistic, humor punctures our phoniness and brings us down where we ought to be.

4. Crouter, *Reinhold Niebuhr*, 124.

Humor can do this without damaging our self-worth. To tell a joke on oneself can be a form of self-love, just as teasing and bantering can be a way of showing love for another person. (Teasing can also get out of proportion and have the opposite effect.) Until my depression took over, humor helped me to not get caught up in my role as pastor. It's helping me again now. When I see myself falling for the temptation to overper-form, take more responsibility than is appropriate, do other people's jobs (in short, when I see myself acting like God Almighty), humor reminds me of my limits and brings me back down to earth. What good is all my theological wisdom if I set myself on fire!

As my depression closed in, I lost this capacity to use gentle humor to keep myself and my work in perspective. My humor darkened, got angry, and became a knife I could twist into my self-respect. I can see now that it also began to slip out in my dealings with parishioners as a release for the anger I felt at their demands.

A close friend and parishioner of mine named Anne, who was serv-ing as chair of the board of deacons, tried to call me on this. On a cold Wednesday, one week before I was hospitalized, I had lunch with her to begin planning for Maundy Thursday. Anne is a petite woman whose face lights up with intelligence. If I hadn't been so beat up and preoccupied, I would have been looking forward to seeing her, trading stories with her, and having some laughs before getting down to business.

During our meeting, several times I had to ask her to repeat herself. I couldn't really hear her because by this time the buzzing in my ears had started.

"Bob, are you all right? You look really tired. To be honest, you've seemed this way the last couple of times we've talked. I know things are really busy at church. I'd be happy to take something off your plate. I never feel that I am doing enough in my position anyway."

"Thanks. I am tired. I worked late last night. It's a busy time. I'm fine. What did you just ask me?"

"I was asking about the service. Do you want me to recruit readers for the verses people say when they snuff out candles? I'd be happy to. Just get me a list of verses you would have them read."

My ears buzzed and my brain pounded so much that I couldn't even answer such a simple helpful question. Finally I said, "Why don't they all say, 'The worms crawl in, the worms crawl out, the worms play pinochle on your snout'? Nobody will know the difference."

"That's not funny. That's not funny at all. Are you sure you're okay?" She had picked up on my sarcasm and on the anger that was behind it. If she had not been a friend and a kind person, she could have made an issue of my response.

I apologized and somehow got through the lunch meeting. All I wanted to do was run out of the restaurant, go home, get into bed, and place pillow tightly over my face. Still a tough nut to crack, I got through the dreadful lunch. Anne asked me again if I was okay. She helped me on with my coat and scarf and walked me over the melting snow to my car. I felt like an elderly man being escorted by his thoughtful daughter. My black humor and sarcasm, expressed so inappropriately, show how completely I had lost all sense of proportion, perspective, and balance. A week later I was in the hospital.

We didn't do any humor therapy in the hospital, though I guess my acting out the word *frantically* was pretty close. What we did do was watch movies, and sometimes movies served that purpose. *Tootsie* did, and so did *Independence Day*. This "Earth vs. Them" classic was one we could all get into. There are some funny lines and some great sight gags in this movie, as when the Will Smith character first starts trying to fly an alien spacecraft and keeps bumping into things. He reminded me of W. C. Fields after a long night at the bar. Even better, in *Independence Day* our side wins. We patients hadn't been on the winning side, at least not recently, and now we had something to cheer about, which we did—wildly.

We also saw *Rio Bravo*, which has turned out to be a key movie for me. It stars John Wayne as the sheriff and Dean Martin as his deputy, named Dude. Dude is a recovering alcoholic. His struggle with alcohol is a major subplot of the film. Ricky Nelson is also in it, which, of course, means that Ricky and Dean get to team up for duets. All of us watching the movie joined in the chorus of "Get Along Home, Cindy, Cindy" and "My Rifle, My Saddle, and Me." We weren't half bad.

My son David was visiting me at the time, and we watched it together: a father–son movie night on the psych unit. A Somali guy sat next to us. He told us that he worked at a camera store and had been hospitalized with PTSD because of fighting in the Somalian civil war when he was fifteen. "I saw this movie in Mogadishu. It was dubbed into Somali. I like it better in English. John Wayne is a real American. There are too many people here who don't want to work. In my country you have to fight for what you want. Fight hard like John Wayne."

For me the most powerful scene involved Dude's struggle to stay sober. One of the bad guys flips a coin in a nearly full spittoon, so Dude has to reach in and get the coin to pay for his drink.

As we watched to see what Dude would do, a young guy in a Twins hat stood up and started yelling at the TV, "Don't do it, Dude. Don't do it. Don't let them take away your dignity. Screw all the bastards. They always try to make you look bad. You don't need the money that bad, damn it. Don't do it."

Dude doesn't do it. Before he can pick up the coin, the sheriff kicks over the spittoon. Later in the movie, Dude gets his revenge by tossing a coin into the spittoon and making the bad guy reach in for it.

The guy in the Twins cap was right; this is a scene about dignity. If you respect yourself, there are certain things you simply will not do. You are worth too much to demean yourself in such a way.

Near the end of *Rio Bravo*, Dude tries to apologize to the sheriff for hitting him during an argument. The sheriff tells him, "'Sorry' don't get it done, Dude."[5] This is classic John Wayne. To practice self-respect is to take the consequences of your actions, to pay the cost. Just saying you're sorry doesn't get it done. But there are things you can do to show you are truly sorry. Those actions will get it done. By the end of the movie, Dude has paid the cost and redeems himself. But he couldn't have done it without the friendship and tough love of the sheriff.

When the movie ended, it was time for David to leave. The click of the door behind him reminded me sharply of what I had lost. I wanted to go home. I went over and sat with Anna. I watched as two guys I didn't know played poker for pieces of jigsaw puzzles. Maybe because it was close to bedtime and we were munching hospital cookies, we started talking about the snacks our moms used to make when we were kids. I told her how my mom used to roll out pie-crust dough with her red-handled rolling pin, slice it into rectangles, and then bake it until it had just the right golden brown color. Sometimes she'd put sugar on the rectangles, sometimes cinnamon, but I liked them best of all when they were just plain.

Anna said, "My mom used to enjoy her bedtime snacks. I can remember my mother and grandmother sitting in the kitchen at night with the kerosene lamp on. They had a tub of butter or even lard between them. Not store butter, but butter that my mother had churned. They'd

5. *Rio Bravo*, DVD, dir. Hawks.

scrape saltines across the top of the butter and sit there munching on the crackers. They both worked so hard that neither one of them ever got fat."

We told other food stories, and soon there were only a couple of people left in the social room. An elderly man who had been admitted that afternoon had fallen asleep in his chair, snoring loudly, leaving a half-eaten ice cream bar melting on the table in front of him. A nurse came over to him and asked if he wouldn't be more comfortable sleeping in his room. As she held his arm, he walked zombie-like, his head bowed down and his whole body sagging. Another day came to an end on the psych unit.

CHAPTER 6

Recovering Choices

DURING MY FIRST COUPLE days in the hospital, I really didn't attend to what day it was. But pretty soon, reading the paper each morning and watching TV got me back on track. So when I woke up Sunday morning, I knew exactly what day it was: Palm Sunday! One of the most important Sundays of the year, and I wasn't in church. I hadn't even checked to make sure the palms had been ordered. Would somebody remember to put a single palm leaf in each bulletin as was our custom? Who would organize the parade of the kids with the palms? Would they remember to keep some of the used palms to make ashes for next year's Ash Wednesday?

I did know that there would be somebody in the pulpit. The day after I had been hospitalized, Sue called Anne and my congregation's president, Joan, to tell them what had happened and also to tell them that they would have to find someone to cover for me while I was in the hospital. We have several ordained ministers who are members of the congregation.

At my request, Sue was totally open with the church leaders about what had happened to me, and she gave them permission to tell the other members of the church. I don't know why, but from the beginning of my hospitalization I chose to be honest about my depression. Maybe I was being bravely honest, doing my part to end the stigma some attach to mental illness. On the other hand, maybe I just wanted to make sure people knew that I had a really good excuse for not showing up at church. I don't know. I do know that I never considered fudging it.

Still, missing Palm Sunday is huge for a pastor like me. I have always liked preaching on Palm Sunday, especially using the line where Jesus responds to the Pharisees who want him to make his disciples shut up: "I tell you that, if these should hold their peace, the stones would immediately cry out" (Luke 19:40). I like singing the verse from the Palm Sunday hymn "Ride on, ride on in majesty. / In holy pomp ride on to die."

I also have a great Palm Sunday children's sermon where I teach the kids signals for sounds. I pull on my ear and they shout, "Hee-haw!" I scratch the top of my head and they shout, "Hosanna!" I rub my chin and they shout, "Alleluia!" Sometimes older parishioners join in. There's nothing like seeing a church choir, mostly people of a certain age and then some, pulling on their ears and then shouting, "Hee-haw!" For UCC folks this may be as close as we get to spiritual frenzy.

I couldn't help but watch the clock. Ten o'clock, when church started without me, triggered all my anxieties. What next? Would I be back for Easter? It sure didn't look like it. How could I possibly not be there for Easter! How many Sundays was I going to miss? Would I ever be back? My fears began to feast on me. What do my parishioners think of me now? Was our insurance really going to pay for my hospitalization? Did we have enough money to pay all our bills with me not working? One question kept coming back to me: When are they going to let me out?

Missing church on Palm Sunday focused my ambivalence about being on a locked psych unit. I needed the unit as sanctuary from demands I could not cope with. But I felt imprisoned and wanted to get out. My Palm Sunday panic pushed me hard toward wanting out. Dr. Anderson had the key to my future. I had to convince him to discharge me. And right on cue, he showed up after lunch in his signature blue blazer and khakis. I didn't waste any time telling him that it was already past time for me to be discharged.

"Slow down, Bob. This is a nonpunitive democracy. If you want to leave, you can leave. You're not on a hold any longer. I think that you're almost ready. Let's just give it a day or two more to make sure that your meds are okay and that things have settled down. If we rush it, we might spoil all the good work you've done."

Rush it? How long was he going to keep me locked up! I was frustrated, disappointed, and angry. I just couldn't get past the fact that he held all the power and I was some kind of supplicant. What could I do to make him let me go home?

When I started paying attention again, he was talking about frogs. "The old frog sits at the bottom of the well and looks up at a circle. When he looks up, sometimes the sky is black, sometimes it's blue, sometimes it's raining, and sometimes there's a moon. From time to time clouds pass over or stars come out. This is his life. The young frog sitting beside him says there's got to be more to life than just this circle; so he hops up on a ledge and then to another ledge, and finally he hops out of the well and into the world." While telling this part of the story, Dr. Anderson made little hopping movements with his hands, like kids at church who accompany a children's song with motions.

"We can learn from that young frog, Bob. There are times when we need to take a risk, learn new behaviors, so that we can enjoy the world." He picked up his coffee mug, studied it, and set it back down in the same place without drinking any coffee. "Do you know why I am telling you this story, Bob?"

I couldn't keep the impatience out of my voice. "Yeah, you think I need to learn new behaviors to enjoy my life. That way I can jump out of the hole that I've gotten myself into. But I've been learning new behaviors ever since I got here. I've talked to you, been to group, and talked with other patients. I think that I have learned what I can. Now it's time for me to be discharged."

I have always been good at interpreting and then applying parables, including those a lot less obvious than his. In fact, I learned recently that Dr. Anderson had plagiarized this particular parable. Far from being his original, it goes back to the Chinese philosopher Zhuangzi (370–311 BCE).[1] I still believe that the knight-and-machine-gun parable is a Dr. Anderson original. Then again, I have bought into his practice of playing fast and loose with the date of Christmas.

He replied, "That's true. When you go back to your church, it's important that you use what you've learned here. If you try to do the same things the same way, you won't get any better. You might even end up being readmitted here. Changing old behaviors is difficult, but it's necessary, and the risk is worth it. You've taken a lot of risks here, and I believe you have made a lot of progress. Why not just rest today? Tomorrow we'll make some decisions." He grinned. "Even God took a day off to rest."

"Yes, God rested on the Sabbath. And I've rested for four days. I've had enough rest. It's time for me to start back to work. I'll be careful to make the changes you suggested and not to do too much too soon."

"Good. If things keep going well, tomorrow we'll make a plan for your discharge. I've got to go now. See you tomorrow, and take it easy today."

1. Armstrong, *Twelve Steps*, 122.

I felt a little better. Tomorrow would be the day. Sue would drive me home. I'd probably take the rest of the day off, and then be back in the office Tuesday morning to work on the Easter service. Well, maybe I'd just stop by the office tomorrow afternoon to check mail and messages so that I'd be ready to get going on Tuesday. With my back-to-work plan now complete, I took some time to make notes on what Dr. Anderson had said and then went out in the social hall to read and hang out.

That afternoon Sue and David came up. By then I had earned purple-level privileges, which meant that I could have gone outside. But, as is so often the case in Minnesota, spring was taking its own sweet time in coming, so I opted instead to go to the hospital dining room, drink coffee, and get caught up on family business. David and I played tabletop football. As I remember it, I won.

After Sue and David left, I spent some more time thinking about Dr. Anderson and his frogs. It's a variation on the story of the guy standing in the corner with his face to the wall. He thinks he's stuck and can't go any place, like the old frog at the bottom of the well. Of course, all that he needs to do is turn around, see all the open space in front of him, and realize that in reality he has lots of options, lots of paths he can take.

Dr. Anderson had done his best to point out to me that I also had options, but to take advantage of them I had to make changes, fundamental changes in my life and work. It wasn't just a matter of turning around and stepping out of the corner. Like the young frog, I had to do some hopping, do the hard work of letting go of the past and choosing a healthier future. At the time I had no idea how hard this work would be.

Palm Sunday afternoon we had a treat. There was no recreation or study group, but there were dogs. It was time for canine therapy. It also turned out to be humor therapy. We went to the recreation room, where the dogs and their owners were waiting for us. All the dogs were small, not pit bulls or Great Danes to really give us a thrill. I had to admit that the dogs that they did bring were kind of cute: several toy poodles, a Pomeranian, and a couple of miniature schnauzers. The dog owners introduced themselves and told us that about once a week they visited a hospital or nursing home. The dogs were even friendlier than their owners, offering themselves to be petted and coming close up to sniff our crotches. (Being on the unit, we could have probably gotten away with sniffing back, but all of us refrained.)

Dottie kept petting and nuzzling a miniature schnauzer. She said, "You know, I had a dog growing up. Not a purebred like this little guy, but a mutt, kind of like the dog with the black circle around his eye in *The Little Rascals*. She'd always be waiting for me when I got home from school, and she slept at the bottom of my bed. She got hit by a car out on the road when I was in third grade. My brother and I buried her in the backyard. I read something from the Bible, and we said the Our Father. I cried and cried. My father told me that she was just a dumb animal and not worth crying over. He teased me and said that I should grow up and act my age. I never had another pet after that, not even a fish or a bird. I still think about her. I still miss her."

She patted the schnauzer while it licked her hand and wagged its tail. Dottie wiped her eyes and smiled at me. "Dogs stick by you. Once you've made friends with a dog, you have a friend for life." Then she grinned, "Not like you fricking men."

The owner of one of the poodles had the dog jump through a hoop for a treat, jumping back and forth again and again as fast as it could go. The dog was jumping its little heart out, but I wasn't at all impressed. I preferred my cat, which doesn't jump through hoops for anybody. While I was thinking about the jumping poodle, one of the guys whispered to me, "I'll bet you a buck that one of these mutts takes a dump on the carpet before this is all over."

"I don't think we're supposed to bet in here. But if we could, I'd put my money on the one that Dottie is holding. It's got a defecating look in its eyes."

"You're right. It looks ready to go. And what about that poodle jumping through the hoops? I thought that only people were supposed to get manic."

In spite of our hope, no dog did its business on the recreation carpet. Dottie cried as she said goodbye to the miniature schnauzer. When my son Tom, who lived on the East Coast, called that night, I told him all about dog therapy. If we had it again, he asked me to put a dollar down on the jumping poodle to take the first dump. I also told him about Jack in the group, and he promised to put some tae kwon do on him if he ever bothered me. I have two great kids.

We never had canine therapy again, so I couldn't place Tom's bet. I'm sorry about that. The more I think about it, the more I am convinced the poodle would have been the first one to go. But at least Tom made his choice and was willing to put his money down. This is the thing about choices, what I think Dr. Anderson was trying to tell me: it's one thing to begin to realize that you have lots of options; but it's another thing, and a much harder thing, to pick one and put your money down on it.

I read somewhere that making a serious choice is like having an amputation. It requires that you cut off all other options. For someone like me in my depression, exhausted and fearful of making a mistake, how could I do something so hard and so final? No wonder I procrastinated like those two old monks Kathleen Norris mentions in *Dakota*, who spent their lives postponing leaving the monastery.[2] But as the saying goes, not to choose is to choose. By not changing, I stayed with the status quo. Fine, except that the status quo included all my old, inadequate ways of coping.

Yes, I had lots of options in my profession and in my life. But it had been horribly difficult for me to take the next step of making one choice and living with the consequences. My self-respect, as well as the whole enterprise of getting on with my life, required me to do just this. Of course until I did, all my options did not make any difference in the real world. They existed only in my head. And if I procrastinated long enough, stayed stuck in a hopeless status quo, then at least I would earn the epitaph "He died with his options open." Big deal.

As my depression deepened, I lost the capacity to make even the easiest choices. I remember one night when I could not place a simple order at Bunny's, my favorite bar, the one where I started hiding in the afternoons. Making such a simple, routine choice suddenly paralyzed me. At church, where the stakes were higher and the choices harder, choosing terrified me. I couldn't think clearly about my options, didn't have the energy for it, and didn't have either the will or the courage to actually choose anything. I just tried to hang in there, avoid all I could, and somehow cope with the rest.

Like my recovery of pleasure, the recovery of my power to choose began my first day on the unit. Granted, this recovery was slight, but it was a start nevertheless. Again it involved food. I had "Chef's Choice" for my first two meals on the unit, but I was given a menu to fill out for the next day's meals. I whizzed right through the breakfast choices: No, I don't care for Ovaltine; and yes, I wanted bacon and anything that I can put syrup on. The rest of the choices were also easy. Yes, I did want fries with that; and no, I didn't want stewed prunes or any other manifestation of prunes, for that matter. As far as I remember, I never chose wrong the whole time I was in the hospital.

2 See Norris, *Dakota*, 6; and chapter 1, pages 5–6, above.

Granted it's a little harder to choose how I am going to live the rest of my life. Talking with Dr. Anderson, visiting with Anna and other friends on the unit, sorting through the feedback I received from my group all helped me to find a new way of making choices. As odd as this may sound to someone who has learned healthier ways of decision making, until my hospitalization I never thought about talking over my important decisions with others. What a relief it is to do this now! It's like getting friends to help you carry something heavy. It's just so much easier to share the burden, this weight of responsibility for a serious choice.

Likewise, when you talk over your choices with others, the choices feel less absolute. So you choose wrong; people make mistakes. It's not the end of the world. Wrong choices need not damage your self-respect. Honestly admitted, as Joan Didion says, they can enhance your self-respect. Choices aren't amputations after all, not most of the time anyway. Life goes on. Admit your mistake; cut your losses; then put your money down a second time. Sometimes you just have to choose something so that you can move on. At least you've closed off an option, and that in itself is learning and progress.

To do this you have to trust other people, to be genuinely open to their influencing what you choose. In my marriage and family life, as well as in my church life, I had always gone through the ritual of consulting and sharing. People expect one to do this kind of due diligence, or whatever. But in reality, this was all phony: I had already made up my mind. I believed that the responsibility was all mine and hence the decision was all mine.

I regret this. Clearly I did wrong to claim sole responsibility and sole authority to make decisions that impacted other people's lives, sometimes even more than my own. I have made other people's lives, as well as my own, harder than they had to be. It's the sin of pride motivated by fear. I apologize and will make amends as I can.

A collateral benefit of sharing decision making is that then others know what you have decided to do and why you have chosen to do it. Understanding what you're trying to do, they can join the crowd cheering you on in the great race to make the best of your life. When I used to run marathons, knowing there were friends on the next corner waiting to cheer for me gave me that extra energy I needed to keep going. If not for me, I kept running for them.

But even with all the help one can get, making life-changing decisions—practicing new ways of coping as Dr. Anderson wanted me to—is very hard. A scene in the movie *Blazing Saddles* shows how hard it is to make life-changing decisions.

In the movie the people in the small western town of Rock Ridge are trying to save their community from a horde made up of "every vicious criminal and gunslinger in the West."[3] These include "rustlers, cut throats, murderers, bounty hunters, desperados, mugs, pugs, thugs, nitwits, half-wits, dimwits, vipers, snipers, con men, Indian agents, Mexican bandits, muggers, buggers, bushwhackers, hornswogglers, horse thieves, . . . , train robbers, bank robbers, ass-kickers, shit-kickers and Methodists."[4] (Apologies to my Methodist brothers and sisters, but substituting *United-Church-of-Christ-ers* for *Methodists* just doesn't flow.)

To tell the truth, except for the Methodists, this list reminds me a lot of a UCC congregation that I once preached to as a Sunday morning supply pastor. One guy had to be a hornswoggler, and the ushers looked like vipers to me. Another guy, dressed mostly in purple and wearing his Vikings horns in honor of our football team, was definitely a mug with nitwit tendencies. His matching wife had fake golden braids hanging from beneath her horns. They both seemed to have gotten an early start on their pregame beer drinking. I've never been back to that church.

Back at Rock Ridge, the salvation of the good citizens of this troubled bit of paradise comes down to whether they can lead all the criminals and gunslingers into a trap. To do this, they have to build a complete replica of their town a few miles away. (The complete suspension of disbelief is quite helpful in enjoying this movie.) To make it still harder, they have only one night to build the town. The upstanding citizens gather in the local church to make their fateful decision.

Of course it falls to the town's preacher to tell the people how dire their situation actually is. At the critical meeting, with the town's fate hanging in the balance, the preacher stands up in front of the townspeople and takes it to the Lord in prayer: "O Lord, do we have the strength to carry off this mighty task in one night? Or are we just jerking off?" And the congregation says, "Amen."[5]

The people have an option, a chance to defeat the hornswogglers, pugs, and all the other bad guys and gals. But they just can't stand around talking about it. For the option to mean anything, they have to choose to

3. *Blazing Saddles*, DVD, dir. Brooks.
4. Ibid.
5. Ibid.

do what that choice requires. And they have to do it together. Otherwise, as the good pastor said, they are just jerking off. Inspired by the pastor's forceful preaching and apt metaphors, they decide to build the replica town. The next day, ready and waiting in their fake town, they take the bad guys and gals totally by surprise. They bushwhack the bushwhackers.

There is sound theology beneath the comedy. The pastor was absolutely right to take it to the Lord in prayer. Yes, the growth of one's self-respect strengthens one's ability to make decisions, to live out those decisions, and to accept the consequences—which, of course, further strengthens one's self-respect. And yes, involving other people in making the decision is a great help; sometimes it is essential, as for the pastor at Rock Ridge. But first, for people of faith, it is essential to bring the decision to God and to try to hear what God has to say about the options.

Some of the psalms have beautiful and moving words about how one does this.

> I will lift up mine eyes unto the hills, from whence cometh my
>   help.
> My help cometh from the LORD, which made heaven and earth.
> He will not suffer thy foot to be moved: he that keepeth thee will
>   not slumber. (Psalm 121:1–3)

> Trust in the LORD, and do good; so shalt thou dwell in the land,
>   and verily thou shalt be fed.
> Delight thyself also in the LORD; and he shall give thee the de-
>   sires of thine heart.
> Commit thy way unto the LORD, trust also in him; and he shall
>   bring it to pass. (Psalm 37:3–5)

I have had the honor of knowing folks whose faith is so strong that they live in a continuing dialogue with God, always praying for guidance and help. Having prayed, they make their choice and leave the outcome in God's hands. Likewise I have known other people who have worked very hard to have faith and yet doubt that God is going to help them even if they commit their way unto God. Like doubting Thomas, they need to see it and feel it in order to trust it.

I wish so much that I were one of those folks with a strong faith. But truly I am more like doubting Thomas. Even as I pray and ask for guidance and help, there is part of me that holds back because of doubt. If I were really honest, I'd ask myself, "Aren't I really asking God to make an exception for me, even if it means that God must violate God's own laws of nature?" But without these laws, how can I predict the outcome of my actions? At least I am good at baffling myself.

Then again (from what I have learned about quantum physics, relativity, black holes, Higgs Bosons, and the like), the so-called laws of nature are a lot more mysterious, unpredictable, subjective, and generally topsy-turvy than what I learned in high school physics. Who can predict what will happen?

If you are like me in my struggle with these brain teasers and conundrums, then I hope you will be helped by some of the things that have helped me to turn to God in prayer, even while fully acknowledging my doubts and questions. Once again the great trust I place in the authors of the Psalms, because of their honesty about pain, helps me. If in the midst of great pain they yet believe that God can help them, as they in fact do, then I am much inclined to believe the same. I know they got the pain right, so that I suspect they got the praying right too.

Also of great help to me has been the father's prayer in the ninth chapter of Mark. He wants Jesus to heal his child from what appears to be a particularly out-of-control kind of epilepsy. The father explains his son's symptoms.

> ". . . but if thou canst do any thing, have compassion on us, and
> help us."
> Jesus said unto him, "If thou canst believe, all things are possible
> to him that believeth."
> And straightway the father of the child cried out, and said with
> tears, "Lord, I believe; help thou mine unbelief." (Mark
> 9:22b–24)

After the father's impassioned cry, Jesus heals his son. I'm not surprised. Jesus cut those in need lots of slack. For him, sincerity and passionate seeking meant far more than conventional piety. He would take the father with his honest unbelief before the Pharisee with his pat answers. I hope that Jesus will understand me. I believe that he does. I want faith badly. I need the hope that it brings to my life. I seek faith and hope with all my heart. Help my unbelief, Lord.

In the Psalms, those who cry out to God often do so because they are tormented by enemies:

> For dogs have compassed me: the assembly of the wicked have
> enclosed me: they pierced my hands and my feet.
> I may tell all my bones: they look and stare upon me.

> They part my garments among them, and cast lots upon my vesture.
>
> But be not thou far from me, O Lord: O my strength, haste thee to help me.
>
> Deliver my soul from the sword: my darling from the power of the dog. (Psalm 22:16–20)

> Lord, how are they increased that trouble me! Many are they that rise up against me.
>
> Many there be which say of my soul, There is no help for him in God. Selah.
>
> But thou, O Lord, art a shield for me; my glory, and the lifter up of mine head. (Psalm 3:1–3)

For me, the dog is the depression that rose up against me. For you, it may be something else that pierced your life and left vast pain. Whatever the cause, these verses acknowledge our pain, as well as our fears and our losses. They state the pain honestly and then, like a prayer, they take our pain to God. For me, these verses are truth that doubt cannot touch.

In *Speaking of Faith*, Krista Tippett writes about her service as a chaplain on Wooster II, the Alzheimer's and dementia floor of a home and hospital for the elderly: "I have always been invested in ideas, in words, in the presentation of words. The people on Wooster II took me out of my head."[6]

This is the paradox of the helper, and it is not a logical game. It is fundamental to our lives. It is simple, and we know that it is true. It goes like this: the people we help also help us, often more than we help them. I think that this is true for at least two reasons. First, our self-respect grows when we help another person. True, we can end up like Job's comforters, doing more harm than good, but only if we refuse to be honest with ourselves about our motives for helping. People with self-respect are honest about their motives, and therefore they can help other people.

Second, as Tippet points out, when we help other people, we get out of our own heads. Helping frees us from our minds and brings us back into life-giving reality. Jesus put the paradox of the helper into these words: "For whosoever will save his life shall lose it: and whosoever will lose his life for my sake shall find it" (Matthew 16:25).

Tippett goes on to say,

---

6. Tippett, *Speaking of Faith*, 112.

> Our cultural debates about the New Testament by way of movies, books, and popular scholarship focus almost exclusively on the historicity and factuality of aspects of the biblical story. But the essential knowledge they describe has only ever made sense— and become authoritative—when it is lived and embodied.[7]

I have learned that to live is to choose to embody our knowledge and beliefs in action. When we have the courage to act, our self-respect grows. When we act to help another person, our self-respect grows all the more. When we act to help another person with such intensity that we forget about ourselves, we save our lives.

After a forgettable movie, Dottie, Anna, a new patient named Mike, and I sat around a table, eating hospital-provided Lorna Doones and talking about a variety of topics. We got on the subject of what we could do to lift the spirit of the people on the unit. Couldn't we think of something that would be fun for everybody?

Starting there, we quickly got to the subject of food. Mike said he had a friend visiting the next day who'd be happy to bring in any kind of food we'd want. We surveyed the affordable options: McDonald's, Burger King, KFC, Subway, and pizza. None of them seemed special enough. Mike and I just couldn't get our minds around Anna's suggestion of lard bread.

"Yes!" Mike suddenly erupted and pumped his fist in the air, just as I imagine David doing after he got Goliath right between the eyes. "I know exactly what we're going to do. It will be great! I'm going to have my friend bring in trays of sushi. We'll have sushi night on Unit 20."

"Wait a minute," Anna said, "I've never had sushi in my life. I'm too old now to start eating raw fish."

Mike answered, "Oh, come on, Anna! Life is short. What have you got to lose that you haven't already lost anyway? Besides, not all sushi is raw fish; there's California rolls and lots of kinds of vegetable sushi. You don't mind raw carrots, do you?"

Mike's enthusiasm drew me in. "Mike, I'm hoping to be discharged tomorrow, but I'll put up half of what you think it will cost." I felt a little sad that I might not be there. I really liked him and his whacked-out idea. It would be fun to be there to support him and to see how it all worked out.

---

7. Ibid., 60.

Mike went into a monologue about the best sushi restaurants in town. The more he talked, the more the scope of his proposed sushi night expanded. He decided we needed to get enough sushi for the staff as well as the patients. We needed seven trays. He'd have his friend buy them at a local supermarket where the sushi wasn't great, but it was quite acceptable and a lot less expensive than getting it takeout from a restaurant. The trays would include a mix of sushi: yellow fin, shrimp, salmon caviar, and as many different kinds of vegetable sushi as possible. Mike agreed to pay the other half of the bill. Anna said she would donate some nuts for appetizers and Dottie said that she would do the same with some of her M&M's.

To be honest, I wondered if Mike actually had such a friend. And if he did, could he pull it off? Would the hospital allow it? Would his alleged friend get the order right? My daydreaming was interrupted by a female patient yelling into one of the wall phones that were available for patient use. "You think that you are a goddamn player. Well, you're just a piece of shit. I've had it with you. Do you hear? I've had it with you. You think you're so fucking cool. You're a fucking loser, and I don't have time for losers like you. I mean it this time. You go to hell, you son of a bitch." She slammed the phone down and slid down the wall sobbing. Mike got up to go over to her, but a nurse got there first, squatting down and putting an arm around her. Together they walked over to a table and started to talk.

I felt like the spectator at a car wreck—so much pain. I gave Mike thirty-five dollars for what I guessed would be my share and told him again that I hoped to be discharged the next morning. The same nurse who had been talking to the woman previously on the phone came over with my pills. She told me that she had been watching me and was impressed with how well I got along with the other patients. We talked about our families, our jobs, and her church. She told me that she felt I deserved a break and a vacation from years and years of hard work. She encouraged me to do the parts of my job that I really loved and get other people to do the other tasks. I liked her, but I felt a little uneasy that she had been watching me.

Happy Palm Sunday.

CHAPTER 7

Sushi Night on the Psych Unit

DR. ANDERSON SHOWED UP the next morning about half an hour later than usual. He had on his psychiatrist uniform and was carrying a mug of coffee. We went back to my room and sat down.

"The coffee isn't all that bad today," he observed. "You know most Scandinavians like weak coffee served scalding hot. I prefer my coffee cooler and stronger." He took a sip of it, as if to make his point. "I saw a robin this morning. Of course it could have been one that hung around all winter. But it feels like spring is finally taking hold." He set the mug down on my end table. I didn't recognize the name of the drug company on the mug. He killed a little more time and then got down to business. "So how are you feeling today?"

In the conversation that followed, I certainly made my case to be released, but I wasn't as anxious about it as I had been our previous session. Palm Sunday had passed, and I felt less urgency about getting back to church to prepare for Easter. One more day wouldn't really matter. Besides, I have lots of old Easter sermons in my file. It's always pretty much the same message anyway.

Dr. Anderson told me that he thought I was ready to be discharged. I thanked him and told him that I would like to be discharged right after breakfast the next morning. I hadn't planned this out, but I had gotten caught up in Mike's plans for sushi night and just had to stay and see how it turned out. In a few days my community had shifted from my church to the psych unit. Besides, I could still make it into work tomorrow afternoon.

"Fine, Bob, like I said, this is a nonpunitive democracy. Tomorrow will be fine. I'll make sure the paperwork is all ready for you. There'll be some papers for you to sign later on today at the nurses' station." I thought we were done with our visit when he blindsided me.

"Bob, after you are discharged, I'd like you to come back and be in the hospital's day program for the rest of this week and then next week. You'll spend the night and weekends at home, but you'll attend the program during the day. You'll have a therapy group and classes, which will give you a chance to go a lot deeper into cognitive-behavioral therapy. I think that the day program will help you consolidate what you've learned and continue your recovery. It will give you a little more time to get well. I'd like you to consider it as a full-time job and not do any church work until you're done. Maybe take a little vacation afterwards before you do go back. If you do go to the day program, I will continue to be your doctor and see you every day while you are there."

He could have smacked me. My body tensed, and I heard that old familiar buzzing sound in my ears. There goes Easter. What had I done wrong? Why was he doing this to me? Hadn't I tried really hard? Hadn't I done everything that he asked me to do? But I had failed, and I had to come back. It would never be over. What more surprises did he have in store for me?

Obviously he picked up on my distress, "Bob, it's okay whatever you decide. My thinking is that it's been only a few days since you were hospitalized. You came in here pretty inert. You see, I think it would help you if you took some time to practice what you have learned before you go back to your church. You've spent your whole life learning one way to respond to what people say, and you've had only a few days to learn another way. Under stress we often revert back to our old ways of coping. I think that the day program would help to ensure that this doesn't happen to you. But I'm okay with whatever you decide."

While we talked back and forth, I was carrying on a parallel conversation in my head. Did he think I might crumble when I went back to work? Was it part of his job to try to sell me on the day program, like a car salesman peddling rust proofing? What would Sue think? What would my parishioners think if I took still more time away? Would our insurance cover it? The one thing I didn't really think about was whether I needed the day program.

Finally, I gave him a preacher's answer that he couldn't refuse, "I'll pray about the day program and let you know what I decide." Screw you. Let him tell me I don't get to pray on it. He's on my turf now. Let's see how he does.

"I'll respect whatever you choose. You know that during the time we've been meeting, I've treated you more like a colleague than as a patient. I'm sure you are a good minister to your congregation."

"Thank you." Immediately I felt guilty for thinking such ill of him. He had blindsided me with the day program, and now he's blindsiding me with kindness. What am I supposed to make of it all? I just sat for a minute, practicing being still, and then said honestly, "You've taught me some things that I really needed to know. Maybe I'll see you in the day program. I didn't know anything about it, and I'm surprised. I just need to think about it and get used to the idea."

What a good guy, even if he was shilling for the day program. He said that he had treated me like a peer. I believe that he did, a feast for my self-respect. Of course I know that I am a sucker for compliments. I needed to talk with people in my church and with Sue to see if she thought it was okay. I needed help in making such an important decision.

I smiled as I thought about this, because I knew that Sue would remind me that at first I always say no to anything new. It's a reflex.

"Want to buy some absurdly expensive trees to plant in the backyard so we can spend all summer watering them?"

"No!"

But after I think about it, I might change my mind—though in this particular case, I think not. I'm not all that flexible, and I'm not good at surprises. But I am getting better. After all, I have had quite a few surprises these last few years.

Also I have to confess that there was a part of me that felt relieved. I wanted to go back to church, and I didn't want to go back to church. I felt that I should want to go back, and that the longer I put it off, the harder it would be. But at the same time, I feared what would happen when I did. Had I learned enough to cope with all the demands of my job, with all the things that had driven me into the hospital in the first place? Dr. Anderson was offering me a respectable way to postpone going back. Why not take it? Who at church could argue with my taking more time in order to get treatment that my doctor said I needed? And who knows? Maybe I would learn something useful. So I was inclined to go to the day program, though it felt wrong to admit it.

I got to group late. Not surprisingly I found it hard to focus. I needed time to sort through all that Dr. Anderson had said, and to think about what I was going to do. When I started to pay attention to what was going on in group, a new patient with a short gray beard and a worn purple robe over his hospital pajamas was talking.

"I've been a bad boy. I went to an auction sale and spent $32,000 on two new cars. When my son found out, he was so mad he put me in here. I'm hoping that he will come today and let me out."

"Harold, it's not completely up to your son," Eric said. "We can talk about it later in group if you want to. Sometimes new patients like to wait a day. It's up to you."

"I'll let these good people do the talking unless I have something that I need to say."

Several people asked for group time. I stayed lost in my own thoughts for a while until Dottie started talking.

"Sometimes I feel like shit because that's the way I get treated. But that's what my boss and my jerk ex-boyfriend want me to feel. They want to see me down. But I refuse to give them the satisfaction. The main reason I want to get well is so that I can say 'Fuck you!' to them. Excuse my French. I know that you people are trying to help me, but I'm not going to let anybody tell me what to do."

I thought to myself, you got that right, Dottie. I know how you feel. People are always telling me what to do. Ever since I was a kid, I've just done what was assigned, made an A on it, and then waited for somebody to give me the next assignment. Now people are telling me I get to choose, that it's a nonpunitive democracy. How am I supposed to know what I want? I want to get well, feel good, and enjoy the rest of my life. Would somebody please tell me what to do?

Several people spoke, and the group did quite well without my participation. Lydia told us about another visit with her son and how well it had gone. She was going to be discharged that afternoon and would move in with her mom. She felt scared but believed that she could handle it.

Eric told her, "I know I've said this before, but nobody is a perfect parent. All parents make mistakes. The best we can do is to try our best."

"I know, but the baby is so small and helpless. I'm so afraid that I'll do something wrong or that I'll just cry all day like I did before I came here." Several members of the group tried to support and comfort her.

Next Eric invited Emily, a new group member, to speak. Somewhere in her early forties, she had a pleasant face and long straight black hair. She told us that she was a piano teacher and performer. She loved playing but was having a hard time performing in front of groups. She spoke so softly that you had to lean forward and listen carefully in order to hear her.

"It's getting worse. I don't even like going into a store. Somebody might start a conversation. I even have to rehearse what I'll say to the cashier in the checkout line. I'm so disappointed. This is my third time here. I thought after the last time I'd be okay. I went back to teaching, even started playing in a combo. One night I got into a cab to go home. I looked at the driver, and then I tensed up. He looked just like my dad. I made him stop at the next corner. When I got home, I OD'd."

She was quiet for a moment. She looked up and brushed her hair back. "My father abused me in every possible way. Some men remind me of him, and I freak out. Post-traumatic stress disorder is part of my diagnosis. I also have major depression. That's why I was late. I just could not get up. My doctor has tried lots of different medications. Some help for a while, but then I'm back where I was. My doctor is having me try something new."

"What's that?" Dottie asked.

"Electroconvulsive therapy. I had my first treatment yesterday. I felt like the shock erased part of my mind. There are things I'd like to forget, but I'm afraid I'll lose my music. It's the one thing in my life that I love. If I lose it, I'll die."

"How did you feel when the treatment was over?" Eric asked.

"I was thirsty and tired. At first I didn't know who I was or where I was. I felt that I needed to start learning things all over. But my thoughts got clearer as the day went on."

"Did anybody give you a choice about treatment?" Norman asked.

"Yes, kind of. My doctor recommended it, since nothing else was working. I decided to do it. I need help with my depression, phobias, and PTSD if I'm going to be able to face life again." As she talked, tears slid down her face, but she kept eye contact with us.

"Emily," Eric said, "I know you are afraid. I just want you to know that I've seen patients helped by ECT. They've said some of the same things you've mentioned. It's a very brave decision to make."

Jack looked at Emily. "Would you play something for us?"

"No, I can't. I'm too tired."

"We're all equal here," Dottie said. "Nobody will hold it against you if you don't play, but I would love to hear a song too."

Emily got up and sat down carefully at the piano. She didn't move. Then she put her hands on the keys, took them off, and then touched the keys again. Then she began to play. I knew the song: "Killing Me Softly." When Emily was finished, she just sat there looking down at the keys. Dottie got up and put her arms around her. Eric said that we were finished.

Emily broke my heart. For a while after group, all I did was think about her and her unbearable pain. How much can one person suffer? A Scripture passage floated to mind: "A bruised reed I will not break." Emily was a broken, bruised reed. Did she have a chance in the world? So much pain had been dumped on her. God, please help her.

"For my soul is full of troubles; and my life draweth nigh unto the grave. I am counted with them that go down into the pit" (Psalm 88:3–4a). Of all the laments, this is the only one that does not offer hope. It starts in the night and ends in darkness. I offer it as a kind of Kaddish for Emily. I hope it isn't necessary.

Anna, Mike, Dottie, and I had lunch. Anna and Mike were not in our group, so we did not talk about Emily. Soon Mike had us fired up again about the sushi. He told us that his friend was bringing eight trays, not seven. He said, "It's probably a lot more than enough. I've been known to overdo it. I just can't wait to see what happens when he shows up with the sushi."

As Mike talked, I realized how much I was looking forward to our sushi party. Before my depression, I had tried to follow the rule told to us in seminary by an old pastor: to survive in ministry, always have something on the calendar that you are looking forward to—not something that you are supposed to look forward to like a denominational conference on communion wafers, but something that you really want to do.

I had long since stopped following his advice. Now, once again I was excited about something. Could we really pull off the clandestine sushi delivery and give everybody a good time? I couldn't wait to find out. True, I would need another dose of Ritalin to be as excited as Mike, but by preacher standards, I was pretty pumped up.

Mike told us that he was worried the staff members might confiscate the sushi. Anna didn't think so, as lots of people shared food that friends brought. The sushi would just be more of the same. Still Mike was worried. Should we tell the staff about it? I advised against it. I quoted a minister's maxim: better to ask for forgiveness than to ask for permission. (Since then, I have abandoned this dangerous maxim.) Finally we decided not to tell the staff. We would just start serving the sushi as fast as we could once Mike's friend showed up—get it to as many people as we could before the staff knew what was going on. We had a plan.

I chose an afternoon group about relaxation techniques. We met in the recreation room with the chairs pushed back. It took some effort, but we were all able to find a place to lie down without touching. As I lay on the floor relaxing, the distinct odor of dog floated over me—bad smell, but a good memory.

In a gentle voice the leader told us to tense all the muscles in our body. Beginning with our feet, she led us through slowly relaxing one group of muscles at a time until finally we came to relaxing the muscles on our necks and faces. Sighs of contentment rose all around me. I have used this relaxation exercise a lot since. Like running, it helps get you out of your head by focusing attention on your body.

After group, those of us in the know hung out expectantly in the dining-room area. We told as many patients as we could not to eat too much because there would be sushi as soon as visiting hours started. Several of them grumbled and told us that they didn't like sushi. One guy told me that sushi sucks and that he wanted pizza. So it goes. On the other hand the hospital unwittingly helped us by serving as chef's choice a tasteless stewed chicken dish with a side of over-boiled potatoes and what looked like yesterday's green beans. Only the chocolate-pudding dessert looked really good.

Mike's friend came through for us! Promptly at the beginning of visiting hours, he showed up with two loaded shopping bags. As soon as an aide let him in, Mike and I rushed over to grab the bags of sushi. We put them on the counter that divides the patients' area from the nurses' station. This is where popcorn and other treats are set out. As soon as we started taking the lids off, the smell of Japan filled the unit until you expected to see Mount Fujimori out the window instead of the hospital's parking garage, and you imagined sumo wrestlers sprinkling salt on the other side of the counter instead of nurses doing their charting.

Mike's friend had also brought a stack of paper plates, a bundle of chop sticks, and some plastic utensils. By the time one of the staff members caught the smell and looked up to see what was going on, we had everything laid out, patients were lining up, and Mike and I were already filling our plates. For most of the patients the fresh red, yellow, green, and orange sushi was irresistible. If the staff wanted to intervene, they'd have to act fast or risk being trampled.

The staff member who first caught a whiff of what was going on was a young student nurse with a Jennifer Anniston haircut. The day before I'd heard a young bipolar guy ask her to marry him. She said no, but she agreed it was okay for him to ask again that afternoon. Now she said, "My God! Look at all the sushi! I can't believe what you guys have done. Is this for everybody?"

I doubt if the hospital had a sushi-night protocol. I do know that the rest of the staff followed her lead. Soon the feast was on. Dottie got her M&M's and Anna got the staff to put her nuts in a bowl next to the sushi. Mohammed, who had a couple of visitors, set out the three liters of Coke that they had brought him. A staff member brought out a bag of Oreos. So we had nuts, mixed sushi, pop, and cookies—pretty much all the major hospital-psych-unit food groups. Nobody got prunes.

Mike picked out a couple of pretty pieces of vegetable sushi for Anna and showed her his way of mixing wasabi sauce with pickled ginger, smiled, and pronounced it good. After a lifetime of eating what she described as cheap chow mein, Anna proved to be adept with the chop sticks. Dottie, a sushi virgin, filled up her plate. "I've had more kinds of drugs than they have on the shelves of a big drugstore. I don't think a little raw fish is going to kill me." I took a plateful and sat off to the side, just enjoying a group of people having a good time.

Secure that the sushi would not be confiscated, Mike asked the rest of the staff to join us. One older nurse, who had the worn look of having seen it all, kept repeating, "Just imagine. Sushi in the psych unit! Who would have thought it?" Mike taught a couple of staff how to mix the condiments. One nurse told us to be careful with any shellfish in case someone was allergic to it. Otherwise, we were green-lighted all the way.

We ringleaders became sushi ambassadors, going from patient to patient, inviting those who held back to give it a try. Several did, and some went to get their own plates. Of course a couple of them were zoned out or asleep. Anna sat down with one elderly woman and put some California roll on a fork for her. It took a while, but Anna helped her eat almost all of it.

I can't be sure, but I think a staff member called her friends on another unit to come and see what was happening. There just seemed to be a lot more people in hospital uniforms than usual. The types of the sushi and the various tastes were discussed back and forth among the patients and staff. The yellow fin got the highest praise; the salmon roe was more take-it-or-leave-it.

A lot of patients got into the spirit of the affair. One guy slapped Mike on his back and said, "Hell of a good idea. This is the best I've felt since they put me in this hole. Can I help pay?" He slapped some bills into Mike's hand. Another added to the store of desserts with a packet of strawberry Twizzlers. Before sushi night, he hadn't shared his stash of Twizzlers with anybody.

An elderly patient I didn't know came up and got a plate of sushi, concentrating on the yellow tail. He turned to us and cracked a huge smile. "I had sushi for the first time in 1945. I was part of our occupation force in Japan. I spent several months as a chauffeur for General MacArthur. Now there's a man who truly was crazy!" At some point a guy brought in a CD, and the staff played it. I expected rap or heavy metal, but it was actually Native American music. Dottie and a guy I didn't know tried to dance to the music. They had mixed results but lots of applause. As other visitors came in, we pointed to the sushi and told them to help themselves.

When Sue and David came to visit, of course the first thing I did was take them over to the sushi. They were even more impressed than I had hoped by what we had done. I called Tom on Sue's cell phone and told him what was happening. He told me that it sounded like there was a party going on in the background. He said that if he had known there'd be sushi, he would have insisted on coming home. I told him how we had plotted and pulled it off without the staff knowing.

"Great, Dad. I'm really proud of you guys."

So for a little while the inmates ran the asylum. But we didn't do it as a power grab, just to give everybody, staff included, a source of pleasure. The staff in their wisdom must have seen how hard we had worked on this, and they did not take it away from us. That night we invented sushi therapy. After supper, at our suggestion, a staff member packed up the leftovers and sent them to the other two psych units.

Like the odor of the wasabi sauce and pickled ginger, the good feelings of the sushi dinner lingered for the rest of the night. A few people watched TV, but most of us just hung out, shaking our heads in disbelief at what had happened. Later I used my purple-level privileges to go to the cafeteria with Sue and David. David said he was buying us some ice cream—Dove bars with nuts, the very best. Life just kept getting better.

We talked over the day program. Sue said that Dr. Anderson had called her about it and that she thought it would be a good idea. She had checked, and our insurance would pick up the whole cost. I was a little taken aback that she and Dr. Anderson had been in conversation, but she had been so straightforward about it. She said she had also talked with Anne and Joan at church. They all felt that it would be a good idea and that, of course, my salary would keep coming. I went with the flow and agreed to go to the day program.

While we talked, Dave read one of his law books. First-year law is hard enough without needing to look after a dad on a psych unit. But there he was. And I knew his brother would drop his life out East and be here with a phone call if I needed him. What a great wife and great kids I have! It had been a long time since I felt so grateful and so hopeful about the future. Again the Psalms gave the words for how I felt: "Happy is he that hath the God of Jacob for his help, whose hope in the LORD his God" (Psalm 146:5).

If I live to be one hundred, and I seem to be getting there fast, sushi night on the psych unit will remain in my top-ten list of lifetime hits. I still can't believe that we pulled it off and that it went over so well. I don't know what has happened to Mike, Anna, Dottie, or any of those folks. I doubt that the nursing student ever married that forever-hopeful bipolar guy. But I just like to think that wherever they are, once in a while they think about sushi night and they smile.

> Behold, how good and how pleasant it is for brethren to dwell
> together in unity!
> It is like the precious ointment upon the head, that ran down
> upon the beard, even Aaron's beard: that went down to the
> skirts of his garments. (Psalm 133:1–2)

Sushi night was good and pleasant, an experience of dwelling in unity in a very unlikely place. I had looked forward to it, my high expectations had been exceeded, and I got to savor it with my family. How could life be any better! Once again Psalm 23 gives words to my reality.

> Thou preparest a table before me in the presence of mine en-
> emies: thou anointest my head with oil; my cup runneth over.
> Surely goodness and mercy shall follow me all the days of my
> life: and I will dwell in the house of the LORD forever. (Psalm
> 23:5–6)

These enemies need not be other people. Enemies can be major depression, bipolar disorder, PTSD, phobias, addictions, poverty, racism, sexism, homophobia, cruelty, and all the other hosts of evil. Think of the list of villains in *Blazing Saddles*, add your nonhuman enemies to it, and then you can start cutting down your enemies by eating sushi in their presence. If you don't have any sushi, no problem. Anything that brings you pleasure in the face of your enemies will send them packing and fill you with joy.

I read somewhere that one reason to believe in God is so that you have someone to thank. I know of no better thank-you to God than these verses from Psalm 147.

> Praise ye the LORD: for it is good to sing praises unto our God;
> for it is pleasant; and praise is comely.
> The LORD doth build up Jerusalem: he gathereth together the
> outcasts of Israel.
> He healeth the broken in heart, and bindeth up their wounds.
> (Psalm 147:1–3)

Sushi night reminded me of why I became a minister. In my official ministerial profile, my professional resumé, I have a long section on my theology of call into the ministry, why I got into this line of low-paying work in the first place. But in reality it boils down to this: I am happy when I make other people happy. And ministers, who are part of many people's lives, have endless opportunities to bring happiness. True, this love of making people happy can be perverted into people pleasing and approval seeking, but acting this way doesn't make me happy. It nauseates me. Eating my sushi and watching so many people enjoying themselves, I was happier than I had been in a long time. Now, if I could only somehow find my way back to making people happy as a paid minister.

After Sue and David left, a nurse came up, thanked me for the sushi, and gave me my pills. Anna had already gone to bed. I said good night to Dottie, and I thanked Mike one more time for his great idea. He was glowing.

My benediction for the day was from two psalms that show us how to live a really good day and what such a day feels like when we go to bed: "Stand in awe, and sin not: commune with your own heart upon your bed, and be still" (Psalm 4:4) and "I laid me down and slept; I awakened; for the LORD sustained me" (Psalm 3:5).

CHAPTER 8

Home

First thing Tuesday morning I went to the nurses' station, signed a few forms, and called Sue to tell her when she should come to take me home. I asked an aide if there was anything for me to put my possessions in, and she gave me three brown shopping bags from a pile in the corner. I wondered if there was some nice church lady out there who carefully saved her shopping bags for us to use on discharge.

In five minutes flat I was packed, including double-checking the drawers and looking under the bed, just as we do when we're staying at a motel. But I did not leave a tip for the maid. And I did not have to deal with the moral dilemma of whether to take (steal?) the complimentary herbal shampoo and green-tea bergamot conditioner. I put the bags on my unmade bed and just stared at them: three brown paper bags were the sole evidence that I had ever been here. Dottie, Mike, and Anna were waiting for me at breakfast. Except for pancakes instead of French toast, breakfast was the same as my first morning on the unit. When Anna picked up her fork, she flashed her fire-engine-red fingernails.

I complimented her on her choice of color. She laughed, "I think one of the aides was trying to cheer me up yesterday or maybe she was bored. Anyway, she volunteered to paint my nails, so now I'm a beauty queen for a day. You see, yesterday started out bad. In the morning I found out that my psychiatrist had filed a petition to have me committed to the state hospital."

"Anna!" Dottie exploded. "Why didn't you tell us last night?" She grabbed Anna's hand. "You owe me. We're friends. You are supposed to tell your friends when something like this happens."

"I know, and I'm sorry, but I didn't want to spoil all the fun with the sushi by bringing up more of my problems. They always keep anyhow."

I asked Anna what was going to happen next and whether there was any way that we could help. She smiled. "You don't need to. My story has a happy ending for once. I learned about the petition from a county nurse who came to interview me. She was a lovely young woman who looks a lot like my niece. We talked for almost an hour over coffee. When she left, she said she'd call my social worker and one of my neighbors in the building to see what they had to say about my ability to cope. She said that there were also a couple of programs that I might be eligible for that would help me. She called back this morning and said that the petition had been denied, so I'm going to stay right here until I'm discharged back to my apartment."

Dottie pumped her fist, "You go, girl! You're the best. Look at those red fingernails. You're a winner. We should be toasting you with champagne instead of drinking this crappy coffee."

From across the room a young patient yelled, "Damn it, I need a smoke. All I want is one lousy smoke."

Dottie yelled back, "And I need a drink. But it ain't gonna happen, brother, so you might as well shut up and get used to it."

Anna took a sip of coffee and looked at me, "Bob, I don't think I'm the only one who has something to celebrate. Didn't I see you walk back to your room with some shopping bags under your arm? Are you being discharged?"

"Yes, I am."

"Can I come with you?" Dottie asked.

I laughed. "Fine with me, but my wife might have a problem with it. I'll really miss you guys. More than anything else that's happened here, you're the reason I'm feeling better and getting discharged."

Anna said, "Bob, you're smart and kind. I've enjoyed getting to know you. I'll miss you. I think you'll do fine when you get home."

"I used to be smart," Dottie said. "I was number three in my high school class. I even was able to play chess. Look at me now. Anna's right, Bob. You're a nice man and a good reverend. I wish I had a reverend like you."

"Thank you, Dottie. I've learned a lot from you. You speak up for yourself. I keep things inside and don't complain. Maybe the next time I start to do that, I'll think of you and put up a fight."

"Mike, thank you for sushi night. It's the best thing that happened while I was here. You know how to get things done. And Anna, I want to thank you for the conversation we had my first day here. Without what I learned from you, I don't think I'd be leaving here today."

"Thanks, Bob. I'll never forget you. By the way, what were you reading that day?"

"Oh, it's called *Fluke*. When we started talking, I was just getting into it, reading about whales and the songs they sing."

Dottie said, "I didn't know whales could sing. What do they sing about?"

"Nobody really knows. It could be a whale version of 'A Hundred Bottles of Beer on the Wall' or some kind of mating song. Who knows?"

Dottie said, "If I was a whale, I'd sing because I had the whole wide ocean to swim around in. What a lot of fun that would be."

The door lock buzzed. I looked at my watch and knew it was Sue. Carrying my three shopping bags of belongings, we went down the same elevator that we had come up six days earlier with Sharon, the admitting nurse, and the guard with the big gut. On the ride home, I went over our insurance coverage with Sue, who assured me yet again that the day program was covered. When I walked into our house, our cat greeted me by rubbing against my leg and then trying to herd me toward her empty bowl. In celebration of being home, I filled the bowl for her. I might as well spread the joy.

The next morning I got up and dressed, putting on my belt and my old running shoes with laces. I don't think I'll ever take belts, shoelaces, or dental floss for granted again. Sue offered to drive me to the day program. We both knew why she offered and why I accepted. She also drove the next day. But on Friday I drove, another step in my recovery. On the way home I stopped at the Electric Fetus (whatever you might think, it's a record store) and picked up a CD that I was eager to hear, one with Roberta Flack singing "Killing Me Softly."

In all I spent a week and a half in the day program, which turned out to be pretty much as advertised by Dr. Anderson. Each day we did a Mood Log, naming our predominant moods and rating their strength from 1 to 10. We also wrote down what we thought was contributing to our moods. These are some examples from my Mood Log.

> Sad 7 and Hopeful 7—Continuing to accept that wellness for me
> will not be a quick fix, even though I feel so much better.

Tired 6 and Anxious 6— I talked about my hospitalization in
group.

Hopeful 8 and Angry 6—I had two conversations about work
in group.

Calm 7 and Anxious 5—This week I'll be completing the day
program and will be working on plans to return to work.

Also on each Mood Log we listed A-talk and B-talk. A-talk is
self-critical; B-talk is self-affirming. The point seemed to be to retrain
our thinking so that when negative A-talk came automatically into our
minds, we would counter it with B-talk. It is a way of changing mental
habits and consequent actions. It is like training oneself to think and act
according to the virtues, as I had been doing with self-respect.

Some examples of my own A-talk and B-talk from my Mood Log
follow:

A-talk: I can't make a decision. B-talk: But I did make a decision
to get help.

A-talk: I'll never get up to speed at work again. B-talk: I don't
need to. Things at work can be changed.

A-talk: I'm a failure. B-talk: I'm dealing bravely with a serious
illness.

A-talk: No progress. B-talk: Progress takes time. Cut yourself
some slack here.

A-talk: People are treating me differently since my hospitalization. B-talk: So what? That's their problem.

A-talk: I'm a failure. B-talk: God doesn't make junk.

Finally on the Mood Log we listed our goals for the day. Again here
some examples from my Mood Log:

To be open, to listen, not to control, at the end of the day to
be wiser about myself, catch up on my journal, consolidate
B-talk and learning.

To read a chapter of Burns' book when I got home.

To learn the different kinds of illogical thinking.

To write five thank-you notes to parishioners.

To reconnect with group after the weekend, to continue to heal
and to talk in group honestly, to say good-bye to my group.

To ensure that we would in fact be safe over the weekend, we filled
out a Weekend Plan with information about where we planned to stay,
with whom we planned to spend time, what we were going to do for fun
and recreation, how we would nurture ourselves, what goals we had for

the weekend, what difficulties we anticipated, and how we intended to cope with those difficulties. It was great to have some plans for fun and recreation over the weekend.

As he had promised, Dr. Anderson saw me daily during the day program. He told me some more good stories, one about greased pigs that I never did understand. Actually I think it was about how the right mix of brain chemicals allows our thoughts to kind of slide over one another, like greased pigs, but this parable is open to multiple interpretations. One day I was stunned when he showed up in a pink shirt, but there was no deep significance. He told me that all his blue shirts were in the wash. The first few days I ran into a couple of people I recognized from the unit, but no one I knew well.

Then when I showed up Monday morning, my fourth day in the day program, there was Mike! When we saw each other, we grinned and hugged like two old friends meeting by chance in a foreign city. He told me that Dottie had been discharged but Anna was still there, though she believed that she would be discharged back to her apartment in a day or two.

On Tuesday Mike wasn't there. The group leader wouldn't tell me much, only that Mike had a problem with his meds and was back on the psych unit. I never saw him again. When Dr. Anderson came that afternoon, I told him about Mike. He put down his coffee cup, one that I recognized, and he asked me how I felt about Mike going back as an inpatient.

"I feel terrible for Mike and his family, and I can't do anything about it. I really like him. He was nice to me and helped me get better. He's such a confident guy, a real doer. I just can't believe he didn't make it. He's a lot stronger than I am. If he can't make it, how can I ever expect to get well?"

"Bob, there are always bumps on the road to recovery from any illness. Maybe this is just a temporary setback for Mike. We don't know. I'm not his doctor, and I couldn't tell you anything if I were. But are you okay? Have any of your symptoms returned? Are you able to sleep? To concentrate? To relax?"

"No, none of my symptoms have returned. I have energy, and I'm sleeping okay. Of course I'm drugged out with Cymbalta and Zyprexa."

"Bob, Mike has to deal with his reality and you with yours. Your reality includes completing this program and making a plan to return to your church. I want you to be careful and not try to do too much too soon. Seriously consider working part-time, at least for the first few weeks. Ask for help. Remember that when you are under stress, it's natural to revert to old ways of coping. The more you can make what you've learned part of yourself, the more it will help you with your stress when you return to work."

He picked up his coffee cup. "And there is one thing you can do for Mike. Pray for him."

Mike's relapse jolted me out of assuming that getting well was somehow guaranteed, that I had paid sufficient dues never to be depressed again. This was not the case. Otherwise the day program was a less-intense version of time on the unit. I was able to talk about things that stressed me at church, and I got out a lot of my resentment toward members who throw their weight around and treat me like a lackey. Some of what I told the group I had never said to anybody before. I also rehashed lots of the things I had talked about on the unit. It helps to say some things multiple times.

Some afternoons we had a kind of a free-form discussion, and I was able to tell preacher stories. I got the best laugh from the story about the Sunday I preached a sermon on perseverance, using as a text the passage in Hebrews about the race and the cloud of witnesses cheering on the runners. I told the group that I wanted a strong closing for the sermon, something that would stick in people's minds. What I intended to say was "Never give up. God is with you. Just keep on trucking." Okay, maybe that's not exactly the firecracker ending I was looking for, but said loud enough, it would get the job done.

But instead of saying what I intended, the devil twisted my tongue, and for *trucking* I substituted *fucking*. However, the devil did not interfere with my speaking loudly. Still I could have gotten away with it. People might have thought they misheard. At least I would have had some deniability. But as soon as the word escaped my lips, I was so shocked that I reflexively slapped myself on the mouth, thereby removing any doubt. For years afterward certain parishioners would greet me at the close of service with "Keep on trucking, Bob!" and then break out laughing. Afterwards, out of the corner of my eye, I could see these parishioners explaining to new members what *Keep on trucking* meant at our church. Your sins can indeed live on from generation to generation.

The people in the group laughed hard at my story; some even cheered. They laughed even harder when I told them that the story had an upside. Nine months later the Sunday school suddenly doubled in size. I guess people really do what I tell them to do, and I have a lot more power than I thought.

I was discharged from the outpatient program on the Friday of my second week, and the following Monday morning at nine a.m. I was back in my office at church. The temperature was in the upper fifties, winter was done for good, the sky was blue, and I felt hopeful. On my voicemail there were a number of calls from parishioners wishing me well, and my stack of mail had lots of cards wishing me the same. Somebody had put flowers and a bag of homemade caramel corn, leftover from Sunday's coffee hour, on my desk. There was a note from Alice, a clergywoman friend, wishing me well and volunteering to preach for me Sunday if I needed a little help getting back in the saddle. Thanks, but no thanks.

That night I went to a regularly scheduled church-council meeting. Joan had told me that I didn't have to come, but I felt strong and ready to resume a full workload. This was my plan, as much as I had one, no part-time days or slowing down. Once back to work, I slipped right back into the way I had always done things. Of course I could do it. It was like Dr. Anderson had never existed.

As the meeting went on, conversations ping-ponged around me much faster than I could follow. The words, all the noise and laughter, bore down on me. It was as if I didn't have any skin; the words scraped against my raw flesh. My ears were ringing, my head ached, and I had no idea what to do or what to say. Like a boxer dead on his feet, I just tried to survive a knockout and make it until the bell. I said what I thought I should say and tried to smile. I survived to the end of the meeting, said quick goodbyes, got out the door, and somehow was able to drive home.

I was already done; I just didn't know it yet. For the rest of the week getting out of bed, taking a shower, brushing my teeth, finding socks that kind of matched—all these little things brought me to the edge. When I stopped at my coffeehouse to kill time before work, I ate my scone without tasting it. Even the always-reliable Mark Trail didn't interest me. Still I made it to Saturday morning, when anxiety finally knocked me down for the count. How could I possibly stand up in front of those people tomorrow? I'd rather die. Thankfully Sue wasn't home, so I could bang my head as much as I wanted.

Thank God I remembered Michelle, a therapist and former member who had moved to the outback of a St. Paul suburb. She had written me a card with a note to call her if I ever needed to. Frantically, I dug through the basketful of cards people had sent me until I found the one with the cat playing with a ball of yarn. Inside was her message and her various phone numbers. I called her home number, and she picked up. I tried for a couple of minutes to be social before I just blurted out how bad I felt. The more I talked, the less coherent I became.

"Bob, are you safe? Do you want me to come over there? I want you to promise me that you won't do anything to hurt yourself."

"I promise, but I can't go on. I can't face church tomorrow, and I can't face not being there. I'm up against the wall. I'm going to let everybody down. I can't believe I'm doing it all over again."

"Is there anybody who can cover for you tomorrow?" I told her about the offer from my friend Alice. "My God, Bob, call her as soon as we hang up! You're not ready to go back yet. You need time to heal. If you had heart surgery, would you be going back so soon? You're not letting anybody down. Nobody who knows you would think that. You're just not able to do it yet. You need to look after yourself. You're so kind to other people. Now is the time for you to be kind to yourself. Would you ask anybody else to do what you're trying to make yourself do? Would you be this demanding on another person?"

"No, I guess not. I just feel so bad."

"You're trying to make yourself do the impossible, like somebody trying to run a marathon right after surgery. You can't preach tomorrow. You're not ready. I know some of the people at your church. They'd never want you to do that to yourself. If you like, I'll make the phone call for you."

As Michelle talked, my breathing slowed down and the pounding in my ears lessened. She had taken charge of my life and given me a plan. I promised her I'd make the call and promised her I'd call her back as soon as I did. When I called Alice and told her I wasn't ready to be in church, she thanked me for the opportunity to help and said that I'd accomplished a lot just going into work for the past week. Her words were balm. I called Michelle back and told her what had happened. She got me to promise I would call her again on Sunday.

Sunday morning I watched the hands of the clock as the time for church approached. I paced back and forth and used all my resources to fight against how bad I felt. With Sue's support and comfort, I made it through the morning. I called Michelle, who sought repeatedly to reassure me that I had done the right thing and that I needed to keep putting my health first.

Around suppertime, Joan called and asked if I would like to meet with a few members of the church leadership on Monday evening. She was quick to say that the meeting was solely for my well-being and that all decisions were in my hands. I knew the people, and I trusted in their love for me.

Sue offered to drive me to the meeting, but I felt that I needed to do that myself. We met in Joan's living room, a comfortable, peaceful space with no overhead lights on. Unlike the church-council meeting a week earlier, now I felt safe. Joan offered me a cup of herbal tea. I tried to calculate: it had been less than a month since Sharon had offered me herbal tea my first night in the hospital.

After some chitchat, a church trustee who was also a therapist said, "Bob, we think you are a wonderful minister who has given more than twenty-five years of your life to our church. Most of us are there because of you. Now we'd like to thank you. We'd like for you to take the next three months for you and Sue to do whatever you like. We'll continue your salary and benefits. We'll look after things at church for you. We just want to give you time to heal so that you can make a hearty decision about whatever you decide to do in the future."

I had not expected this. But there was one thing I had to tell them before I accepted their gift. "Thank you. I know that I'm not ready to go back to church. I want to, but I just can't. I'd like to take the three months away from church, but I don't know if I can accept your offer because I might decide that I can't ever come back." Maybe not the clever thing to say, but I had told the truth.

"We know that," she said. "For now we just want to give you time. Use it for yourself. You've helped to create a strong church. Don't worry about us. Trust us. Our offer is our gift to you. We hope you will accept it."

I did.

Against the depression trying to destroy me, here stood a multitude of good people offering me grace. With them watching over me, I could say with the psalmist:

> The LORD is my light and my salvation; whom shall I fear? the
> LORD is the strength of my life; of whom shall I be afraid?
> When the wicked, even mine enemies and my foes, came upon
> me to eat up my flesh, they stumbled and fell. (Psalm 27:1–2)

Depression, so eager to devour my life, could not stand up against those whom God had sent to protect me.

So, doubter that I am, do I really believe that God was active in my life, working through people who loved me in order to save me from depression, my mortal enemy? I want to say yes, but I think of all those who don't make the life-saving phone calls, all those who take their own lives. Why didn't God help them? I've grown a lot in faith since my initial breakdown. But I think there will always be this unanswered question: Why me? Why save me and not them? Job was outraged by his undeserved suffering; I am troubled by my undeserved grace. Of course grace is undeserved. That's why it's grace. But why me and not all the others?

It comes down to this: the doubts that I keep running into, here and in other places, don't keep me from faith, but they do mean that I have to keep working at my faith. I can never take my faith for granted. Maybe it is a good thing that there are at least some ministers like me. When parishioners come to me to talk about their doubts, it's easy for me to empathize and to understand.

If I could write my own psalm about this, I would start by being honest about my doubts: Why do some not make the phone call for help? Then I would ask God to help all those in need, to give them hope. Then finally I would proclaim that God is my own hope, my Strong Deliverer. Until I find words to write my psalm, I sustain my hope by reading the psalms that I didn't write.

My three-month grace period gave me time to reflect on my hospitalization. Indeed, I lived with my hospitalization daily as I turned my written notes into a manuscript. The three months also gave me time to sort through the rubble left from my failed attempt to return to my church: Why had I disregarded Dr. Anderson's counsel about returning to work gradually? Why had I not developed a serious plan to avoid a relapse? Why couldn't I cut myself some more slack?

In these months I found a good balance between this work and just having fun. They were like the weekend plan I had while I was in the day program, but these days extended through the summer. We took some short trips, watched lots of movies, and mostly loved the life we led. I enjoyed good food and listened to good music. Our son Tom came home for a visit, and the four of us took a canoe trip on the St. Croix River. Absolute bliss, time for a psalm of joy:

> O come, let us sing unto the LORD: let us make a joyful noise to
>   the rock of our salvation.
> Let us come before his presence with thanksgiving, and make a
>   joyful noise unto him with psalms. (Psalm 95:1–2)

As I relaxed more, I started to see that for a long time I had been treating myself like some kind of machine, maybe like one of the cars that Dr. Anderson had talked about. I broke down and ended up in the hospital to get fixed, just like as a car that doesn't run ends up in a garage. I got my new set of spark plugs that I needed to be a good runner again and headed back to work.

Since I had been repaired, why couldn't I immediately stomp on the accelerator and get back to top speed? My almost-immediate breakdown showed the danger of this kind of thinking. Flesh and blood have limits, and they need healing time. Michelle was right: recovering from depression is like recovering from heart surgery. It is certainly not like auto repair.

I thought about Dr. Anderson's stories and about his telling me that he had been treating me as a peer. In his work with me, I believe that he had tried to balance my need to fully recover with my need to go back to work. I believe he was afraid that if I took too long to go back to work, I would never return. In the day program and in groups that I have been part of subsequently, I have met people who have chronic depression, who have not been able to return to whatever their work had been. I fear that Anna might be one of these. Each depression is different, but in my case, I believe Dr. Anderson felt I could go either way—hence his telling me to take it slowly in my return to work, and his never questioning that I would go back to my church.

During those months of recovery, I also had the help of both a psychiatrist and a therapist. My psychiatrist, Dr. Park, dressed with a lot more variety and style than Dr. Anderson, but he did not look a bit like Sigmund Freud either. We met for twenty minutes once a month for a three-way interaction: him, me, and his laptop. We always talked about my medications, which now included BuSpar. In addition, we talked about my moods and general mental status.

He didn't waste any time. How could he, with my HMO-allotted twenty minutes ticking away? Once, when I told him I was afraid that the medications might be damaging my memory, he immediately asked me to start counting backwards from one hundred by sevens. I did it, and that was sufficient for the immediate diagnosis of a sound memory. He is fast and extremely good at what he does.

I started off seeing Alan, my therapist, for fifty minutes once a week, and then we met every other week. Straightforward and unpretentious, he was somewhere in his midfifties. He reminded me of a shorter, slightly balding version of Jimmy Stewart—an "Aw, shucks," therapist. He dressed even less formally than Dr. Anderson—sport shirt, no tie or jacket.

On my first visit to the clinic where he worked, I sat in the waiting room, surreptitiously checking out how crazy the other patients looked. Alan called my name, and as he led me back to his little office, he asked me if I wanted a cup of coffee. I accepted, establishing a ritual of coffee offered and accepted, which we have reenacted at most of our visits since. A small thing, but he had gone out of his way to fetch the coffee for me. Would somebody who was just there for his paycheck do that? As I waited for him to return, I looked over all the books on his bookcase. The titles certainly didn't bode well: sexual abuse, divorce, alcoholism, sexual dysfunction, shame, and suicide. I couldn't have all these problems, could I?

In our first sessions, I used my hospital stories like good sermon illustrations to keep the sessions interesting and myself in control. But soon things started to drag. Alan didn't seem impatient or bored, but I was aware that the hands of the clock on his bookcase had stopped moving. I started to panic. Nothing I could think of to say was funny, insightful, or worth his time. I was keeping him away from other patients who really deserved his help. I dug my fingers into my palms and apologized to Alan for wasting his time. "Why do you feel you're wasting my time, Bob?" We had started.

If Dr. Anderson was a hare, Alan was a tortoise: no leaps of insight, no parables or Zen koans to be pondered for deep meaning—just careful listening and the right questions, again and again and again. Slowly he helped untangle the emotional knots that I had gotten myself into. Like the Psalms, he is honest about shame, guilt, fear, and anger. His calmness started to rub off on me. He heard, never judged, and he always encouraged me to say more. I don't mean that he was passive. He had a way of going back to previous sessions to make connections that helped me see the wider picture. With his gentle guidance, I was able to keep on trucking through therapy.

I still have a note Alan wrote me: "My father doesn't get to decide for me anymore." Of course I knew how big a role my dad played in my life, but Alan helped me to sort out the major role that he continued to play. I was able to get some of the hurt out, and Alan helped me to not feel guilty and disloyal when I did.

We talked a lot about shame. He asked me to read John Bradshaw's book *Healing the Shame That Binds You,* in which I learned about "toxic

A Pelican of the Wilderness

shame."[1] This happens when, as you are growing up, you are taught that just being yourself is inadequate and unacceptable. Toxic shame echoes what CBT calls labeling: you don't make mistakes; you are a mistake. By being shamed in this way, you lose touch with your own life—who you are and what you want. No wonder it became so hard for me to make decisions. Ultimately, toxic shame leads you to become a "false self," living not for yourself but for the approval of others. This requires lots of energy, and ultimately it can be exhausting.[2] I know.

The danger of labeling and toxic shame are things that I needed to know in order to survive. As Reynolds Price writes in his novel *Roxanna Slade*:

> From my long past what I've mainly dwelt on when I looked back for consolation are six or eight instants when I learned a thing I badly needed to know for survival or when I glimpsed a lone child or adult performing some act of open-hearted grace in no hope at all of the smallest reward.[3]

In my recovery, I have experienced open-hearted grace from an admitting nurse, from a Somali housekeeper, and from other mental patients—from those who had no hope of any reward from me. I have glimpsed God in them.

Toward the end of *Rio Bravo*, Dude (Dean Martin) has lost his fight with the bottle. With hands that won't stop shaking, what good is a gunfighter to anybody anyway? At least when he's drunk, his hands stay still. So he pours himself a drink and slowly brings it to his lips. But before he can taste it, he hears trumpets playing "Deguello." The music means that the outlaws plaguing the town will show no mercy to Dude's friend, the sheriff. Dude stops, listens to the music, looks at his still hands, and pours the liquor back in the bottle. "I didn't spill a drop. The shakes are gone just because of a piece of music. Until they played that piece, I forgot how I got into this."[4]

In the voice-over commentary on the DVD, this scene is called "The Redemption of Dude." The music, coming just at that critical moment, was the immediate agent of redemption. Was it an accident, just pure randomness, or something else?

1. Bradshaw, *Healing the Shame*, 9–10.
2. Ibid., 14.
3. Price, *Roxanna Slade*, 43.
4. *Rio Bravo*, DVD, dir. Hawks.

CHAPTER 9

Too Much Too Soon

TOWARD THE END OF the three-month gift of time from my church, Joan, the congregation's president, called. We talked for a while about how the summer had been for us and our families. She filled me in on how things had been going at church. Alice, my clergy friend, along with our remarkably skilled seminarian, had managed things while I was away.

She also said that while I was away, the church leadership had learned for the first time just how much I had been doing. As a result, they had hired someone to do part of the building-management work I had done, especially looking after several groups that rent space at the church. I had been the flack catcher and go-between for the church and these groups, a part of my work I hated.

"That's right. We've needed three people to do what you were doing all by yourself." She laughed. "With what we have learned, we'll try to do our jobs better and take some responsibilities off you. I don't want to rush you, but pretty soon we're going to need to know what your plans are so we can decide how to move ahead. Maybe you'd like to come back part-time. If you do, why don't you start around July 15? Things should be quiet with the summer schedule. If you don't feel that you are ready to come back then, the church would arrange for further pastoral coverage."

I thanked her for her thoughtfulness, emphasized again how well I felt, and said that I was ready and eager to come back on the fifteenth. We agreed that I would work part-time through the summer. It was a good conversation.

Three days later I was back—back in the hospital. The morning after Joan called me, I lay in bed with a pillow tight over my face. I kept pounding on the pillow as hard as I could. When Sue finally got me up, I could not stop repeating, "I'm an asshole. I can't stand myself. I can't believe what I just did. I was home free. Now I've screwed everything up again. I can't stand it. I can't do it. I just can't do it. Why in the hell did I say that I was going back? I'm going to kill myself." I hit myself hard on the temple, hard enough to make a bruise. I kept hoping Sue would run an errand so that I could go and bang my head against the shower wall. Maybe I'd get lucky and fracture my skull.

As I raged against myself, Sue kept telling me how much she loved me and how none of what I was saying was true. She pleaded with me to stop. She said that if I couldn't stop my ranting, she'd have to take me back to the hospital. For two days this is how we lived. She didn't dare to leave me and go to work. I started breathing rapidly and sighing so deeply that I was moaning. I tried to use my CBT skills, tried to think of what Dr. Anderson and Alan had taught me, tried not to disappoint my friends on the unit, but nothing helped. Like a child playing in the sand, I lined up all my little pebbles and shells on the beach against a tide that was fast coming in. The pebbles and shells were the techniques that I had learned to stay healthy; the tide was the depression. No chance and no way.

On the third day Sue made an emergency appointment with Alan. She went with me and held my hand while I waited. I concentrated on breathing normally and not sighing too loudly. With no opening coffee or chitchat, Alan asked me what was wrong. I tried to minimize what was happening, but soon it just all poured out. He listened, nodded, and quickly offered me a tissue when I started to cry. I don't believe I have ever felt worse in my life; I was a bruised and now-broken reed.

He didn't try to argue me out of my feelings. He told me that he was concerned for me, that I definitely was not ready to go back to church, and that I should think seriously about going back to the hospital where I would be safe. We walked back into the waiting room to talk with Sue. It was after 5 p.m., and most people had gone home. But Sue, my psychiatrist, and my psychiatrist's nurse were all waiting for me—an impromptu intervention. With care and sadness, they each told me that they believed I needed to go back to the hospital. I cried but knew I had no choice; once again matters had been taken out of my hands.

Once I gave up, things went smoothly. Going downhill is easy. My psychiatrist was able to get me a room on the unit, so I could avoid the ER with its attendant miseries. Sue and I stopped at the house, where I packed my hospital pajamas, a notebook, and my copy of *Moby-Dick* (a follow-up after finishing *Fluke*). I even found the cat and stroked her goodbye. She didn't seem all that concerned.

The nurse who admitted me on the unit was friendly enough and said she recognized me from my previous stay, a mixed blessing. She took me to my room, this time a double, and apologized as she went through the things in my traveling bag. She said that my notebook would have to be kept at the nurses' station because of its metal spiral, though I could have it whenever I wanted it.

After the admissions procedure, I joined Sue in the social room. I half expected to see some familiar faces, but everybody was new. Showing that I was a vet, I walked over to the refrigerator and helped myself to two cups of vanilla ice cream. While Sue and I ate, I watched the fish swimming lazily in the tank. As I had the first time, once I was in the hospital, I felt the blessing of being safe. I lost all interest in harming myself. Some part of me had wanted to be back on the psych unit. Once again matters that were more than I could handle had been taken out of my hands. I didn't have any more responsibilities than those fish.

After Sue left, I introduced myself to a couple other patients who were watching the Twins lose a game on TV. A teenager in green hospital pajamas and a T-shirt with a picture of laughing Jesus burped loudly, laughed, and said, "From under the floor, up the basement stairs, across the hall, and out the front door." I talked with him during the commercials. He was a sweet kid from Oklahoma with more tattoos on his arms than I could count. He made me happy by being impressed that this was my second time in. He told me that he belonged to a robot-making club, that he was gay, and that he had a very high IQ.

I also talked with an obese teenage girl in a stained black T-shirt and sweat pants. She had compiled a list of complaints against the unit. She wrote terribly, but her complaints were clear enough: 1) Rude attitude of nurses and HUCs (Health Unit Coordinators); 2) Food selection poor and bland, even for those not on special diets; 3) Not enough activities for those who don't have privileges; 4) Not enough games, and all the puzzles have missing pieces. I told her that in my experience most of the meals had been pretty good and that so far I had been lucky with nurses and staff. We were joined by a Tibetan woman who shared her lemon jawbreakers with us. She told us how lucky we were to be Americans.

My roommate turned out to be the teenager in the green pajamas. I am pro-LGBT theologically and politically. I think that if Jesus came back today, gays would be among the first he'd want to break bread with. But a gay roommate gave me pause. He turned out to be perfect. He didn't snore, and once he stopped munching the cookies he brought back to the room, he fell right asleep. He was a little sloppy with his stuff, but I could outsloppy him. He was a good kid.

The next morning, while eating breakfast by myself, I listened to a young man trying to buy a used car over one of the hospital phones. From his side of the conversation, it didn't sound like he was making too much progress. He kept reassuring the would-be seller that, in spite of his poor credit history, he had a good job and could easily make the payments. I took this to be total bullshit, but I couldn't help but be impressed with the chutzpah with which he was playing such a bad hand.

At one point he said, "If I had good credit, I wouldn't be wasting time talking to you." As he talked, he took swigs out of a plastic bottle of Coke and stroked a scar on his cheek. "Shit!" he yelled as he hung up the phone. Then he grinned at no one in particular, "I almost got a car off that fucker. I'll try him again after lunch."

I compared myself with this guy, who didn't have a lot going for him except his glibness. With no good cards to play, he still wouldn't quit. In comparison, I had all face cards, but I had cashed in my hand. My family, several academic degrees, my own home, money in the bank, a pension: I had so much going for me. If this guy had what I had, he'd be king of the world or at least the Donald Trump of Minneapolis. After I put my breakfast tray away, I walked past where he was sitting, drinking his Coke, and reading the for-sale ads. He had circled several of them.

Since there was still time before group, I decided to do some note taking, so I went up to the desk to get my spiral notebook. I congratulated myself for having remembered to grab the notebook as Sue and I were leaving home. At the station, the secretary, or HUC, was doing some kind of paperwork. She looked up, saw me, and went back to her work. Finally I said, "Excuse me." My voice came out a little high.

She continued writing for a while and finally said, "What do you want?"

"May I have my spiral notebook, please?"

"And who are you? I can't get your notebook unless you tell me your name. We have thirty patients on this unit. I can't know the names of every one of you." In this little power game, the clerk had all the aces, and she enjoyed playing them.

Finally I got my notebook. I remembered #1 on the list of the girl with the black T-shirt: "Rude attitude of nurses and HUCs." For the first time I had experienced this fully. Whatever therapeutic milieu hospitals hope to establish for their treatment of the mentally ill, one staffperson who enjoys jerking people around can go a long way toward undoing it.

It helped to remember Sharon, the Somali cleaning lady, the good-humored staff at sushi night, and even the perky nurse with her cheerful suicide question. I'd met so many good people on the psych unit; I wasn't going to give one mean person the power to ruin my day. Besides, I am a resourceful person. When I was done taking notes, I checked to make sure nobody was watching, tucked my notebook under my arm, carried it back to my room, and hid it under my underwear. I never took it back to the desk.

Sitting on my bed, I had the time and finally the peace of mind to think through what had happened to me. During the three months between my hospitalizations, I had been working on what turned out to be an early draft of this book. I had written about my renewed appreciation for pleasure, my need to face reality, the importance of self-respect, getting help in making choices, the spiritual help I had found in the Psalms, and other themes of my recovery. Fine, important things to learn, but they didn't seem to be of much help to me when the chips were down and I had to go back to work.

Did this mean I had been on the wrong track? No, I had enjoyed three great months, feeling better than I had in years. If I had not tried to go back to work, I'd still be leading the good life. But the stress of this decision, my failure to consolidate what I had learned, and my inability to integrate healthy behaviors into my life left me vulnerable to a relapse. I had thought and written about fundamental changes in my life, but I had not made any of these changes. Looking back, the most fundamental change I needed to make belonged in the category of the bleeding obvious, and I was almost ready to make it.

When I returned to the social room, I saw Dr. Anderson in his standard psychiatrist uniform. We walked back to my room together. We sat for a little while in silence, like two old friends just letting it all sink in. He then told me how sorry he was that I was back in the hospital. I told him what had happened in the previous three months. Then I told him about my call from Joan, my agreement to return to work, and my subsequent relapse.

I picked up on his sadness, which fed my feeling that I had let him down. But what could I do about it? I had dutifully taken my meds, gone to therapy and to my psychiatrist, read what I had been asked to read, written all that I could write, and done my best to be good to myself. I had even read the Bible daily. And look what happened to me! How could I have known that agreeing to return to my church would cause my depression to erupt again?

He didn't tell me any riddles and parables; mostly he listened. As I talked with him, the decision was made somewhere inside me, the only decision I could make. Making it felt like sliding the last piece into a difficult puzzle. I would quit. I could never go back to that church again. Quitting is absolutely what I needed to do in order to survive. Of course it was. Once I recognized this, it was like—well, duh!—the absolute bleeding obvious indeed. Yet until I talked with Dr. Anderson, I had not recognized consciously that somewhere deeper inside of me a decision had been made.

I think this decision was made in the same part of me that had decided not to swerve into the tree, to call Sue, and later to call Michelle—the part of me that wanted to go on living. I told Dr. Anderson what was as true as sunrise to me: I had no other options; going back to my church would kill me.

What I have to say about that part of me that wanted to go on living is getting close to soul talk. Parker Palmer, the one who coined the term "practical atheism," is also a survivor of two bouts of severe depression. In an interview by Krista Tippett, Palmer says:

> And yet, as I worked my way through that darkness, I sometimes became aware that way back there in the woods somewhere was this sort of primitive piece of animal life. Some kind of existential reality, some kind of core of being, of my own being—I don't know, maybe of the life force generally—that was somehow holding out the hope of life to me. And so I now see the soul as that wild creature way back there in the woods that knows how to survive in very hard places, knows how to survive in places where the intellect doesn't, where the feelings don't, and where the will cannot.[1]

For me the soul isn't so much "that wild creature way back there in the woods," though I know from my own experience that the soul is beyond one's conscious control. From my experience, the soul is more like the "core of being, of my own being" that even in the worst moments of my life "was somehow holding out the hope of life to me."

1. Tippett, *Einstein's God*, 236.

Without getting into two millennia of theological discussions about the soul, I simply want to say that at that critical moment of life and death I encountered my center, something hard like a pearl, and it saved my life. Underneath my intellect and will, this inner center, or core, kept life and hope alive when all the rest of me had shut down. I call it my soul. My Hindu friends—I once presided at a Christian-Hindu wedding where I did not get to ride on an elephant but did almost fall off a cliff (unintentionally) into the Pacific Ocean—would say that I had touched the God within me. Of course some Christians would say that also.

At any rate, Dr. Anderson didn't flinch when I told him that going back to my ministry would kill me. After we had talked it over more, he encouraged me not to make such an important decision on the spur of the moment.

"Bob, what do you think you're going to lose by not being the pastor of people you have known for so long, by not preaching on Sunday mornings, by not having a regular job that you can count on? You've been at your church for such a long time. I'm asking you to be as sure as you can before you decide to leave."

I agreed that I would bring up my decision in group and also talk it over with my family. I truly wanted their feedback, and I craved their understanding. Yet, it also felt like a done deal—not one of those unclear, maybe-yes–maybe-no decisions where you need others to help clarify your thinking. And I knew that they would understand, probably applaud.

Dr. Anderson also said that if I stuck to my decision, I should contact the right people in my church and denomination about possible disability payments. I love his practical side. "It's your money, Bob. I say, get all you can. That's what I would do." I have done that ever since. It's reality.

I told him that Sue had told me repeatedly that we would be fine financially if I never went back to work, and that the only thing that mattered was my happiness. As I talked with Dr. Anderson, I got the feeling that, like the trustee at that last church meeting, he wanted me to make a "hearty decision." He wanted me to decide from an assured conviction, not out of anxiety: that I had recognized my options and chosen the one that would give me the best shot at happiness. He knew that I needed to be able to look back on this life-changing decision, without cringing in shame, but with self-respect for facing reality and accepting the cost of what I had chosen.

To talk in group about leaving my church, I had to face up to some social realities. I knew that I had so many more options than most of the people there, lots more face cards in my hand. I didn't want to sound to them like I was whining or maybe like I was bragging about how good I had it. Looking back, given that we all had been locked up together, I'm not sure how realistic my concerns were. I worry too much about how I come across to other people and about hurting people's feelings.

Eric, again my group leader, recognized me and gave me a smile when I came into group. I asked for time. When my turn came, I spoke honestly about my depression and what had happened to me in my work as a minister because of it. I especially talked about my relapse when I tried to go back to work and how I needed to decide what to do next. I told them that I didn't think I would go back but that I wanted to know how they felt about my decision.

The feedback was strong and direct.

"You worked for twenty-six years at the same church and now you're tired. What do you expect? After all that time doing the same thing, of course you're bored and have low energy. You're an educated man. Why not do something different for a change?"

"Why are you going back unless you need the money?"

"Excuse me if this is inappropriate, but you look old enough to retire anyway."

"Let me get this straight: The job made you depressed. You don't have to do it, but you're thinking about going back anyway. Why? Do you like being on a psych unit that much?"

One guy in his late twenties did a good job of merging my reality with his. He was so thin that he could have been a serious runner, and he clearly cared about his appearance: he sported an expensive haircut and wore tan pants with a sharp crease and well-shined tasseled loafers. As he spoke, he had the habit of taking his glasses off, polishing them on his bright white shirt, and putting them back on again.

"I know what you mean about not having any energy," he said. "I used to be to be the top salesman at Lexus of Benson, but I'm not in the game anymore. I haven't had my A-game in months, ever since I went off meth. When I first started on meth, I had energy to burn, but I still felt calm and in control. But soon it started going the other way and I was out of control. I promised my mom I would quit meth. And I have, but my life has lost all its glory and passion. I have no motivation. All I want to do is sleep. I slept twelve hours last night. I don't see any point in getting up. Yeah, I know what it's like not to have energy."

Eric brought the discussion back to me and asked me if I had received the feedback from the group that I needed. Yes, I had. The group had helped a lot more than I thought it would. They got me out of my head and into the world with other people. Seeing my decision through the eyes of others helped me to be more at peace with it.

The day before I was discharged, I had breakfast with a new patient. He looked like he could have been a minister himself, but he was an appliance salesman. He told me that he had come in with severe depression and that his wife didn't want their children or anyone at his work to know.

"She's ashamed of me. She's also afraid I'll lose my job if the guys at work find out what happened to me. And she won't let my children visit me here. She's told them that I am in the hospital for tests." He asked if I would like to have lunch with him, but when lunch time came, he was gone.

His story reminded me to count my blessings. We have messed up our share of the details as a family, but on the major things, like my illness, we have been solid in our support for one another. Far from shaming me, my family has encouraged me to be honest about my depression. Far from shaming me, they keep referring to my courage in facing my demons. Far from shaming me, they have helped me to regain my self-respect. But to be totally honest, I have to say that they have also tried to set limits on my behavior. They won't allow me to call myself a loony or a whack job or even to say that I can't take out the trash because I'm too depressed. Good for them!

Later that afternoon I ate vanilla ice cream and read *Moby-Dick*. I had read it many years before and seen the movie in which Gregory Peck is cast as Captain Ahab, one of the all-time crazies of literature caught on film. Like a minister playing out his psychic issues in managing a congregation, Ahab plays out his monomania aboard his ship as he bends the crew to his vengeful purpose. Ministers and whaling-ship captains should read *Moby-Dick* and learn its cautionary tale.

Early on, there is a scene set in the mariner's chapel in New Bedford, Massachusetts, where Father Mapple (Orson Wells in the movie) preaches on Jonah and the whale to a congregation more accustomed to being on whale boats than being in church. After an opening hymn, Father Mapple enters the church and climbs up a rope ladder into his pulpit, which is shaped like the prow of a ship. Then he carefully pulls up the rope ladder behind him. The ship is an ancient symbol for the church; and on this ship, Father Mapple is clearly the captain.

He reads from the book of Jonah, closes the Bible, and tells the story of how Jonah, a prodigal sailor, thought that he could thwart the will of God. The story began when God told Jonah to go to the great city of Nineveh and prophesy in order to save the people from the wrath to come. But because the people of Nineveh were enemies of Israel, Jonah's own country, Jonah did not want them to repent. Rather, he wanted them to endure the full measure of God's wrath. Instead of booking passage to Nineveh, Jonah booked passage to Tarshish, which was in the opposite direction. He sought to escape the Lord, but that proved to be impossible.

In the Jonah story, soon after the ship sailed, a storm arose at sea. Through Father Mapple's words, the congregation heard the mighty wind and felt the spray. They felt the fear of the sailors as each cried to his god when the ship started to flounder in the great waves. Convinced that such a storm could only be the act of an enraged god, the sailors drew lots to see who among them had evoked such anger. The lot fell on Jonah. The sailors tried still harder to reach land, but the tempest was against them. Finally, with great reluctance, they took up Jonah and cast him into the sea. Immediately the waters calmed and the sky cleared.

With his congregation—many of whom knew what it was to be flung out of a whaling ship into the ocean—straining to hear every word, Father Mapple told them that God did not abandon Jonah.

> God came upon him in the whale, and swallowed him down to living gulfs of doom, and with swift slantings, tore him along "into the midst of the seas," where the eddying depths sucked him ten thousand fathoms down, and "the weeds were wrapped around his head," and all the watery world of woe bowled over him. Yet even then beyond the reach of any plummet—"out of the belly of hell"—when the whale grounded upon the ocean's utmost bones, even then, God heard the engulphed, repenting prophet when he cried. Then God spake unto the fish; and from the shuddering cold and blackness of the sea, the whale came breeching up towards the warm and pleasant sun, and all the delights of air and earth; and "vomited out Jonah upon the dry land."[2]

2. Melville, *Moby-Dick*, 63–64.

God had saved Jonah, just as each of the mariners hoped God would save him if the sudden rush of a harpooned whale capsized his whaleboat and sent him into the sea. As the author of Psalm 130 writes:

> Out of the depths have I cried unto thee, O Lord,
> Lord hear my voice: let thine ears be attentive to the voice of my
> supplications.
> I wait for the Lord, my soul doth wait, and in his word do I hope.
> My soul waiteth for the Lord more than they that watch for the
> morning: I say more than they that watch for the morning.
> (Psalm 130:1–2, 5–6)

God heard Jonah's cry out of the depths and delivered him to dry ground. This is the good news of Father Mapple's sermon to the sailors soon to ship out on whale boats: as for Jonah, so for them. God will not abandon them, even in the depths of the sea. God will be their strong deliverer. The sailors left the chapel with their faith renewed, ready for the voyage of perhaps two or more years that awaited them.

Not by the device of a whale but through the help of many people, God had come to me in the depths and had brought me safely home. This is what I believe, even as I struggle with my unbelief. For me and for many others, there is another lesson in the book of Jonah. It is not part of Father Mapple's sermon, but nevertheless it is a message we desperately need to hear in order to survive. Read Jonah to the end—it's a short book—and you'll see that the story is not really about Jonah and the whale. It's about Jonah's refusal to make the sacrifice needed to get on with his life.

I had to sacrifice a job. In the last part of the book of Jonah, Jonah also has to make a sacrifice—not of a job but of an attitude: of his hatred for the people of Nineveh. God does all God can to show Jonah that this hatred is wrong and that it prevents him from fullness of life. God's effort to teach Jonah these lessons begins when the whale casts Jonah up on shore close to Nineveh. Far from escaping God's commission to prophesy to these people, Jonah finds himself right at their doorstep, delivered by God via the whale.

> And the word of the Lord came unto Jonah the second time,
> saying,
> Arise, go to Niveveh, that great city, and preach unto it the
> preaching that I bid thee. (Jonah 3:1–2)

But Jonah still does not want to fulfill God's command. His time in the belly of the whale has not changed him sufficiently. He still holds on to his hatred against these people. Ninevites are his enemies, the enemies of Israel, and he continues to loathe them. However, God has given him no choice; so against his will, Jonah prophesies to the people of Nineveh. Much to his dismay and disgust, they repent and God does not destroy them.

Jonah is so angry that he beseeches God to kill him. So doing, he stands prophecy on its head. Unlike so many of the great prophets of Israel, Jonah has actually succeeded in his mission. People listened to him and changed their ways. Jonah could be savoring his success and asking God for another prophetic commission. Instead, blinded by his hatred and prejudice, he wants only to die.

But again, God does not abandon him. After the people of Nineveh have repented, Jonah goes out of the city and makes himself a booth so that he can have some shade while he watches the city. Maybe they will commit some new sins and God will destroy them after all. It doesn't happen. Instead God makes a gourd to come and grow up over Jonah to provide extra shade. Finally something makes Jonah happy. But the next day a worm comes and kills the gourd, so Jonah loses some of his beloved shade.

To make sure that Jonah gets the point of God's lesson with the gourd, God causes a scorching east wind to arise, and the sun beats down on Jonah's head. Again Jonah tells God that he wants to die. The book ends with God speaking to Jonah:

> Doest thou well to be angry for the gourd? And he said, I do well to be angry, even unto death.
> Then said the LORD, Thou hast had pity on the gourd, for which thou hast not labored, neither madest it grow; which came up in a night, and perished in a night;
> And should I not spare Nineveh, that great city, wherein are more than sixscore thousand persons that cannot discern between their right hand and their left hand; and also much cattle? (Jonah 4:9b–11)

We do not know if the lesson of the gourd is sufficient for Jonah to give up the prejudice and hatred that prevents him from being a willing prophet. He had encountered God in the depths and darkness and also in the dazzling light of the day. Even so, he clutches his hatred and prejudice so tightly that he cannot open his hand and reach out to God, who keeps reaching out to him. Jonah just cannot bring himself to sacrifice what had become so much a part of him, even if it brings him to despair.

In my experience, in order for you to make this kind of sacrifice, reality has to lay such a heavy hand on you that you are convinced there is no other way to go on living. My second hospitalization did this to me. I hope that in the end the same happened for Jonah. I hope that there's a lost final chapter to the book of Jonah in which he accepts the reality of his situation and gives up his anger and hatred. If so, the chapter has yet to be found.

In recovering from depression, one size doesn't fit all. I am convinced that leaving my job was essential to my recovery, but this doesn't mean that others recovering from depression need to leave their jobs. I met a number of people during my two hospitalizations who wanted to return to their old jobs. For them the depression triggers were elsewhere. Work was a source of identity and self-respect.

But others I met in the hospital were more like me. Their work itself had become a depression trigger. If they went back, the odds were stacked against their recovery. Yet out of financial necessity, real or perceived, they felt that they had no choice but to return to their work. If, like me, you are interested in justice for the mentally ill, then a good place to start might be to help out financially those who must return to work but for whom work threatens recovery.

Money helped in my recovery, but it did not shield me from the unimaginable pain of major depression. Richard Rohr, a Franciscan priest, writes in *Things Hidden*, "Pain teaches a most counterintuitive thing— that we must go down before we even know what up is."[3] Rohr goes on to say, "I would define suffering very simply as 'whenever you are not in control.'"[4] I believe this. Intolerable pain forced me down into the darkness and depths. I lost control of my life. I needed this to happen before I was willing to make the sacrifice necessary to know what up was. And now I not only know what up is, I live it.

In *Breakfast at Tiffany's*, Holly has to sacrifice the Tiffany-elegant, superficial life that she has created in order to find the happiness and security she craves. At the climax of the movie she must choose between her life of freedom and noncommitment (her life as a "wild thing") and the love that Paul Varjak (George Peppard) offers her. When it seems certain that she will reject his offer of love, Paul tells her in desperation,

3. Rohr, *Things Hidden*, 25.
4. Ibid.

> You know what's wrong with you, Miss Whoever-you-are? You're chicken, you've got no guts. You're afraid to stick out your chin and say, "Okay, life's a fact, people do fall in love, people do belong to each other, because that's the only chance anybody's got for real happiness." You call yourself a free spirit, a "wild thing," and you're terrified somebody's gonna stick you in a cage. Well baby, you're already in that cage. You built it yourself. And it's not bounded in the west by Tulip, Texas, or in the east by Somali-land. It's wherever you go. Because no matter where you run, you just end up running into yourself.[5]

Holly comes so very close to leaving Paul there in a taxi in the rain, but in the end she goes to him. For me the movie earns this happy ending of lovers reunited before the closing credits. Holly has experienced the shame of living off one "rat" after another, followed by the catastrophe of her brother's death and her rejection of a man who offered her a future that seemed to be financially secure. Life as a "wild thing" has brought her to despair. For a chance at "real happiness," she has to let it go. We don't know if she and Paul find happiness, but I'd give them a lot better odds than I would Jonah.

5. *Breakfast at Tiffany's*, DVD, dir. Edwards.

CHAPTER 10

Losses and Gains

MY SECOND HOSPITALIZATION LASTED five days, followed by two weeks in the day program. Then I was discharged into an uncertain future, which got a lot more certain once my disability checks started coming. Along with Sue's income, my checks kept us marginally in the black. I had passed my fifty-eighth birthday, and though I had not declared myself retired, I didn't plan on going back to pastoral work. Staying out of the psych unit gave me all the work that I needed.

Soon I settled into a life at home similar to how I had lived during the three months between my hospitalizations: working on this never-ending manuscript, watching many movies on Turner Classic Movies, reading whatever I liked, listening to whatever I liked, and enjoying some inexpensive travel, including seeing the world's largest ball of twine in Darwin, Minnesota.

Sometimes a piece of music—the ethereal harmony of the vocal group Anonymous Four or the hard-as-nails realism of red-dirt singers like Lucinda Williams—felt exactly the way I was feeling. Sometimes what I read perfectly caught something that I had learned. For example, a character in Saul Bellow's novel *Herzog* says, "But as one recovers self-confidence, one learns the simple strength of simple desires."[1]

During this time, I also went to regular appointments with my therapist and psychologist and had lunch or coffee and conversation with friends—mostly clergy, but some normal people also. However, early on, I learned that in fact not everyone is comfortable talking with a former mental patient like me. While I was still in the day program, I had run across a clergy colleague who happened to be visiting in the hospital. I

1. Bellow, *Herzog*, 152.

A Pelican of the Wilderness

was glad to see him and made a joke. He recoiled from me. You would have thought the crypt had just opened up in front of him and I was beckoning him to jump in with the rest of us zombies. He muttered a quick "I'll pray for you," half genuflected, did an about-face, and took off walking quickly and stiffly down the hall in the opposite direction.

I asked Dr. Anderson about that encounter, and he laughed.

"He thinks that you're cuckoo, Bob, and that if he says the wrong thing, he might set you off. What would he do then? He'd be responsible for your breakdown, not to mention any property that you might destroy."

From the perspective of that clergy friend, I can see that in our encounter I held the power: mess with me and I'll go crazy on you. I soon discovered, though, that my family is not vulnerable to this form of intimidation.

About three months after I resigned, I took part in a ritual of closure at my old church. This is not mandatory for a pastor leaving a church in the United Church of Christ denomination, but I believe in rituals that mark rites of passage. Besides, there were so many people I wanted to say goodbye to. The ritual includes a liturgy for pastor and congregation in which each party forgives the other for any wrong done in their relationship. This part of the ritual is an honest acknowledgment that no relationship is free of pain. Likewise there are words and prayers that acknowledge all the joy that is part of a pastoral relationship, and other words and prayers that bid Godspeed in the future. It's a good ritual.

This ritual of closure formally ended my twenty-six-year pastoral relationship with my former congregation. I'm glad I took part in the closing ritual, even though it felt a little anticlimactic. My struggle about whether to leave was long past. I had not seriously doubted my decision. When the phone rang, I perked up; maybe it was a friend calling to ask if I wanted to go to a game or movie. For sure, it was not going to be a parishioner with yet another demand. I had no parishioners. Still, I had been at the church so long, and goodbyes needed to be said. I knew that some folks would be quite relieved to see that I was even able to participate without going cuckoo on them and smashing the church's good dishes.

I stayed at the reception following the ritual of closure until the last coffee pot was empty and the last bar eaten. The coffee was two steps above psych-unit coffee, and the bars were excellent, especially the lemon bars with powdered sugar sprinkled on them. There was no sushi. Telling stories and making jokes, I reassured lots of people who needed me to be okay. To be totally honest, I did think about foaming at the mouth a little just to get a rise out of them, but I heeded the saner angels of my nature.

Many parishioners told me how grateful they were for what I had done for them and for the church. A number gave Sue and me cards, which I still read when I need encouragement or just want to remember. I had forgotten what I had done that had really helped people. But the people remembered. We were given a memory scrapbook created by a parishioner and a card with a substantial check in it. (I should resign more often!)

Of all that was said and done for me during the reception, I took to heart most deeply the words of a young parishioner: "Don't forget to brush your own teeth." This young man had gone through a lot of pain in his life, and I suspect that he had heard these words in his own therapy or maybe in a treatment program. I take his words as an injunction to stay close to the real world and to not forget to tend to daily stuff like brushing your teeth.

In *An Altar in the World*, Barbara Brown Taylor urges the importance of a theology based on the awareness and daily care of one's body.

> What is saving my life now is the conviction that there is no
> spiritual treasure to be found apart from the bodily experiences
> of human life on earth. My life depends on engaging the most
> ordinary physical activities with the most exquisite attention I
> can give them.[2]

What is more ordinary than brushing your teeth! Not working, I had plenty of time for the "most ordinary physical activities": cooking, doing the dishes, vacuuming, dusting (largely pointless in my opinion), yard work, and so on. I embraced this with less than total enthusiasm, but I did experience at least partially the blessing that Taylor is writing about. If tasting bacon is my image for enjoying the simplest pleasure, then brushing my teeth is my image for facing the simplest reality.

Brushing my teeth, fully acknowledging the "bodily experiences of human life," also meant taking care and responsibility for the health of my body, to be a good steward of the flesh and blood God had given me. I tried to exercise every day and got into the habit of taking long walks. This felt good. Eating well and enjoying what I ate felt even better. But this was not enough. To care for my body fully, I had to face one of my

---

2. Taylor, *Altar in the World*, xv.

greatest fears. I had to have a physical exam, something that I had not done since seminary.

Of course this is something a lot of people do regularly, often giving the results as much heed as the results of getting their car checked out. But for me, having a physical involved a huge change in how I coped with the world. When it came to my health, I had lived by denial and avoidance, the magic belief that what you don't know won't hurt you. I coped by denial and, I suspect, by some kind of tacit bargain like "God, as long as I'm a nice person and work hard, you won't give me cancer, will you?" I learned this way of coping and the fear that drives it from my mom. Time had passed; I had become an adult, and the time had come for me to give up these childish ways. I, not my mom, now have responsibility for my health.

I faced down my fears, made the appointment, had the checkup, and found out I was okay. So in one sense, it was all a big anticlimax. It was also a great victory. Having that physical was a huge step out of my head and into reality. And I haven't stopped: each year since then I've had my annual checkup. The victory over fear is never completely won, but it does get easier and easier to call and make the appointment. Each time I go in, I tell the doctor that I want every test that my HMO will cover.

Honestly, getting these physicals has engendered more self-respect than anything else I have done during my recovery. I faced up to a gut-level fear and did something about it. People with self-respect, people like me, are the kind of people who don't let fear stop them from doing important things. To pick the obvious example, they don't risk their lives by not going to the doctor.

Also, I started getting mad. Writing about the clerk on the unit who jerked me around helps me own how angry I was with her. I should have told her exactly how I felt about her power games. Now, at least most days, if somebody mistreats me, tries to chip away at my self-respect, I push back. I haven't gotten a permit to carry a concealed weapon, but I now know what anger feels like and I can put it in words that get people's attention.

There is a startling line in Saul Bellow's *Herzog*: "Hatred is self-respect. If you want to hold your head up among people . . ."[3] Herzog had been a doormat for lots of people, and he needed to get his self-respect back. Hatred became a quick fix for doing this. Likewise there's a lot of hatred in some of the psalms. In them, people who had been treated badly give full vent to their anger.

3. Bellow, *Herzog*, 289.

Personally, I don't want to get stuck on hating people; it feels too much like Job. But I am convinced of the redemptive power of anger; for me, anger is truly a component of self-respect. I think of Dude in *Rio Bravo* flipping the coin into the spittoon to satisfy his anger and regain his self-respect. If I had been in that saloon, I would have cheered for him.

As months passed after my second hospitalization, I realized that over the years in ministry I had swallowed a lot of anger. A few of my former parishioners had been way over the top in the demands that they had made on me. They took advantage of me and jerked me around because they could. For many years, I had put on a happy face and let them get away with it. Being away from the church, I could finally admit what they had done to me and how I felt about it. I'll never let anybody treat me that way again.

But these were only a very few people over many years. Like most of the staff on the psych unit, most of my parishioners were good folks, or at least pretty good folks, trying to do the best they could in the midst of their own troubles. As time passed, I realized how much I missed so many of them. I had been at the center of a thick web of relationships, and suddenly I had been cut out of it. Each month when the church newsletter came in the mail, I read every word and thought about every person.

Following the ethics of my profession, I did my best not to interfere with my successor and did not stay in pastoral contact with former parishioners. Facing the end of these pastoral relationships was really hard. Sue and I joined another church, where we were welcomed, honored, and cared for. But there's no substitute for a long history with people. Dr. Anderson was right to make sure that I understood fully what I was sacrificing when I left my church. However, I don't think even he knew that I was sacrificing relationships that in moments of crisis and joy had brought God very close.

I had lunch a few times with a couple of colleagues who also had left churches after long pastorates. We all were struggling with separation from relationships that had given our lives much meaning. We were all glad to be done. We all wished for a little more contact with our former churches, some little thing or other. We all appreciated it when our successors called to tell us about a major event in the congregation—or better yet, when they called to ask us about some history or even for advice.

The talk with other pastors was good. Even better was being accepted as a colleague who had done faithful work. Already my twenty-six years of ministry were becoming more than the story of why I left. As I write this, I am deeply grateful to the current minister at my old church. He goes out of his way to honor my service and my history there. This kindness has helped me to let go, to remember fondly, and to get well.

Also during this time, Michelle, the therapist and former member of my church, made a point of having lunch with me every few weeks. Once she asked, "Bob, will you do me a favor?"

"If I possibly can."

She almost exploded across the table, "No, Bob! No! That's not it at all. You don't even know what I want yet. You don't have to do me a favor just because I ask. Maybe you won't want to. You get to hear what I want and then decide. You can say no. That's okay."

I get to decide.

Another time I told Michelle how stressed I had felt when people in church couldn't get along, and how hard I had tried to make sure that this never happened.

She put down her glass, looked hard at me, and said, "How dare you deprive people of their disagreements! That's so arrogant."

It had never occurred to me until that moment that some people actually enjoy disagreements. I don't need to like these people, and I sure hope that any church I serve won't have too many of them, but it is certainly not my job to change them. It is indeed arrogant to think that I can.

Sometimes something totally random reminded me of a lesson that I could not afford to forget. One morning I went to Anodyne, a coffeehouse where there are huge easy chairs, perfect for reading and writing. It also has the best scones in the Twin Cities. Unlike the coffee shop where I had hid before going to work, it has no bad associations for me, but it does have an extremely diverse clientele, including many LGBT folks.

One fall afternoon I was writing away, oblivious to what was going on around me, when one of the baristas put on a Neil Diamond CD and cranked up the volume. With the first words of "Sweet Caroline," folks abandoned their newspapers, shoved their laptops aside, and forgot their lattes. Stoked up on strong coffee and moved by great music, almost everybody in the coffeehouse sang along.

A few minutes before, we were just a bunch of strangers; now we were the Anodyne Neil Diamond Tribute Choir. When the song ended, after applause and cheers, people went back to their business. But for a few shining moments, we had been to the mountaintop of pleasure with Neil. Like grace or even the Holy Spirit, pleasure is a gift of God that one cannot control.

I'm not sure the Holy Spirit had anything to do with them, but there were times of remarkable synergy in my recovery. In therapy Alan kept emphasizing that, as an adult, I am free to choose, that I no longer have to choose based on what I think will please my dad—or congregants, for that matter. Shortly after this therapy session, I watched *Now, Voyager* on Turner Classic Movies, a movie in which Charlotte Vale (Bette Davis) fights to free herself from her mother, who had always made decisions for her, which—as Mrs. Vale is quick to say—were always the right decisions for Charlotte.

In a confrontation with her mother, Charlotte finally claims her own freedom: "I haven't had independence. Independence is relying upon one's own will and judgment."[4] Then in an internal dialogue she continues, "I'm not afraid. I'm not afraid, Mother."[5] Like Charlotte Vale, I had to learn not to be afraid, to make decisions on healthier, more adult, and more realistic criteria than what would please my dad.

So my life went along comfortably until a session with Dr. Park, my psychiatrist, in the spring of the following year, about eight months after I had resigned from my church. Knowing what I know now, I would have been more wary going into this session. I've learned that if he wants me to make a change, such as dropping or cutting back on a medication, Dr. Park always brings it up in the spring. He's a big believer in the role winter and darkness play in depression, especially in a place like Minnesota, where it's pitch dark in midwinter before five o'clock in the afternoon. When the days are getting longer, heading toward summer twilights that can go on for hours, that's when he believes a person is most hopeful and can best cope with change.

I did not know this about him at the time though, so I was totally unprepared for what he said. Dr. Park blindsided me: "Bob, I think that your recovery has reached the point where you may need more stress in your life." What a bizarre thing for a psychiatrist to say! Isn't his job to reduce my stress, not to encourage me to go looking for more? Is this what I get for a $15-per-session copay?

I'm sure he saw the look of incomprehension in my eyes, though I don't think he was intimidated by my newfound ability to get angry. At any rate he continued. "You know, life is stressful. You can't escape it. That's just the way it is. I think that you've shown that you can cope with the ordinary stresses of life. I think you could also cope with going back to work. Of

4. *Now, Voyager*, DVD, dir. Rappe.
5. Ibid.

course it's up to you. A lot of guys your age cash it in, buy an RV, and take off. Though with gas prices where they are, I'm not sure they get very far."

He went on. "But to me, this doesn't sound like you. I'm not sure you want the position you resigned from to be your last position. I think you might rather retire when you want to, not when events force your hand. I'm not saying go back to work tomorrow or even in the next few months. I am asking you to think about what makes you happy. Of course a lot depends on the position. In my profession there are jobs that are 'locum tenens,' positions of limited duration. Maybe that would be best for you at the beginning."

I told him that I would think about it. You can't really tell your psychiatrist that you won't think about it. I talked the idea over with Sue, Alan, Michelle, some clergy friends, and with UCC conference staff. In all of this I built on the kind of shared decision making that I had first practiced with Dr. Anderson and my group during my second hospitalization. In different ways, everyone encouraged me to do what I thought would make me happy. I would get to decide. They also agreed that if I decided to return to work, I should go back gradually and absolutely not commit to anything that threatened my recovery.

In the past I might have done what I thought would please Dr. Park, the authority figure closest to my dad in the hierarchy. I might also have gotten a yellow legal pad and added up the financial disadvantages and advantages. I might have had a sudden surge of guilt for living on disability when I should have been out there doing the Lord's work.

Not that these old ways didn't assert themselves a little. Yet I did, for the first time in my life, make a collaborative decision that centered on what I wanted to do. My decision to leave the church had been collaborative, but more along the lines of coming to recognize and accept the inevitable. This time I was truly free. I didn't have to do anything that I didn't want to do. I had gone from Oz to Paradise, more or less.

As Dr. Park suggested, I chose to look for time-limited work, what we call sabbatical supply. It usually lasts for three months, while a pastor is on sabbatical leave. The position is obviously time-limited, and it doesn't call for any skills I don't already have. Even if some unhealthy behaviors returned, I knew that I had lots of support. Besides, it was only for three months. Clinching the decision for me was the fact that I simply needed something more to do. It's hard to structure days and weeks without work and without any kind of retirement plan. Escaping boredom can be a positive motivator.

Also, I had something new to bring to my work. If I were a cancer survivor, I would use my experience and the resulting credibility to help others dealing with cancer. Instead, I am a depression survivor, and I can use my experience and the resulting credibility to help others going through depression. When I redeem my experience by helping others, it gives meaning and purpose to my suffering.

In my job searches, I have learned that there is a time and a place for such sharing. In my first interview I made sure that the committee knew not only that I had twice been hospitalized for depression but also that depression is a very serious mental illness. Give me an A for honesty but an *F* for strategy. Actually, if I were less scrupulous than I am, it might have been a great strategy. I could have been playing on the guilt of the good people on the committee, manipulating them into hiring me. Maybe they'd be afraid that if they told me no, I'd go off on them. The committee did not hire me. However, as it turned out, I knew and respected the person they did hire, so the turndown didn't sting that badly.

When I told Alan how the interview had gone, he gave me some reality. "Bob, I admire your honesty. That's part of who you are. But it's up to you to decide how much you want to share in a job interview. Don't apply if you think your depression will prevent you from doing the job. Otherwise, the context of a job interview is not the place to talk about your depression. Of course if they see there's a gap in your résumé and ask you about it, then I know you'll tell them the truth. But there's a lot of depression and burnout in our society. You don't have to make it sound like a catastrophe."

I took his words to heart and got the next sabbatical-supply position I applied for. I did choose to bring up my depression at one point in the interview—I just had to—but the committee chair said that he knew lots of people with depression and that if I felt okay now, that was good enough for him. This church is in walking distance from our home. I'll never forget the day I started working there, kissing Sue as I walked out the door with my brown-bag lunch and little briefcase. Substitute a Howdy Doody lunch box for the brown bag and I could have been kissing my mom as I left for the first day of school.

The three months went fast, and the job went well. Indeed I thrived "like a green olive tree in the house of God" (Psalm 52:8). As I've done in the seven other positions I have had since then, I make it a point to talk about my depression from the pulpit—but I get to pick how and when and for what purpose. And I don't preach a whole sermon on depression. I want people to come back next week.

Instead, when I talk about my depression, I use what I have learned from my depression and recovery to illustrate various points in a sermon: We all have limits and weaknesses. All of us need at times to turn the future over to God. All of us need the help of God and of other people. None of us are perfect. We have innate dignity and worth as God's children. None of us can control other people or the future. Pleasure is far too precious to be taken for granted. The capacity to choose is part of what it means to be made in the image of God. Self-respect is a gift of God. Giving and asking for help is the soul of a community. Obviously I get lots of sermonic mileage out of my depression.

The subtext of these sermons is show-and-tell: First, I show that I, the preacher, have gone through serious depression and now I am back in the pulpit. I may be a little long in the tooth and the sermons may get a little twisted, but I can still reach back and deliver that high, hard sermon. I am as sane as the typical preacher, and I am not hung up on or ashamed about what happened to me. Next comes what I hope is the telling, the applied lesson: if this guy can get well—or at least well enough—so can I, or my wife, my husband, my daughter, my son, my neighbor.

This planned self-disclosure in my sermons has been universally well received. Afterwards people thank me for being open, even for being brave. And as you would expect, during the coffee hour or over the phone the next day, someone tells me that they would like to talk with me about their depression or the depression of someone they love. So I redeem my depression, one sermon at a time.

I have two great stories from my time at the first church I served as a sabbatical-supply pastor. First, one Sunday a not-so-young couple sitting pretty close to the front progressed during my sermon from holding hands, to hugging, to mutual thigh stroking, to mutual higher and higher thigh stroking. Never before have I wanted to say, "Get a room!" in the middle of a sermon, but I was tempted that day. Fortunately they did remain fully clothed throughout worship, which seems like a sufficiently minimum requirement, even for the UCC. There is no lesson in this R-rated story. It's for fun.

Second, at the close of my last sermon the congregation gave me a standing ovation. Better yet, one elderly woman actually shouted, "And he's good looking too!" I have no idea about the current status of her cataracts.

After two more short-term positions that went well, I took specialized training to be an interim minister. With the training, I can serve churches between permanent pastors. Although an interim is for a much longer time than a sabbatical supply, the position is still not open-ended. I have served in four such interims—one for almost two years. The first two were at small-town churches in the heartland of Minnesota. My knowledge of cows has skyrocketed.

I have great respect for the members of these congregations. They work faithfully to keep their churches going, even as their communities lose population. They walk the walk of faith. They have helped to bring out the best in me as a minister. Though like the parishioners in my old church, amidst so many good people, there are always one or two that—to use baseball language—I'd like to trade for a parishioner to be named later.

Each of these interims had its stressful times: challenging staffing problems, financial concerns, building problems, wasps infiltrating the sanctuary from the nest under the eaves. Sometimes I worried, sometimes I had trouble getting to sleep when I knew a parishioner was upset with me, but never did I lie awake at night savagely tearing into myself; never did I feel an urge to relieve the tension by banging my head against a wall.

And most of the time I had fun, using the skills and experience I had gained through a long career. I have enjoyed the work, the people, and all the new learning that comes when a city boy lives in a small town. I even won a bingo game during Bear Days, the community festival in a small town where I was serving. For the sake of total disclosure, I have to say that when I won, I pumped my fist and shouted "Yes!" so loudly that I frightened the little girl sitting next to me. Later a kind elderly parishioner informed me that it is customary when one wins at bingo to say "Bingo!" loudly enough to be distinctly heard but not so loudly that small children are frightened. I keep on learning new things.

To ensure that I keep things in perspective and do my best work, now I have a group of valued colleagues I can openly discuss problems with as issues emerge in my work. They respect my skills and my commitment. I respect theirs. I can be honest with them when I don't know what to do. I'm not ashamed to admit mistakes or overly bashful about owning my successes. I can do this in good part because I am mostly able to avoid personalizing. Again, it's not about me; it's about the church that I serve. And to serve well, I need to consult with colleagues. To me, this is much like getting an annual physical: simply something adults with self-respect and self-confidence do.

I tell my colleagues that I've just about figured out how to start doing ministry.

CHAPTER 11

Recovery

Now, more than eight years since my hospitalizations, I know that I have been "patched, retreaded and approved for the road."[1] God willing, I will live well with my depression deep into my social-security and pension-collecting years. I hope so. I want the money, and my life is far too satisfying to let go of it any time soon. I live well, but I also live with depression. I know that relapses occur, as they tragically did for Sylvia Plath, author of *The Bell Jar*, the source of the above quotation.

I can go through a week packed with numerous church meetings, even tedious and unnecessary ones, and still feel grateful that I can once again practice my profession. I might feel tired and frustrated at times, but I also know the feeling of having done good work. In the midst of a busy day, I can put my own concerns out of my mind and listen carefully to the hurt of others. I can serve effectively in the wider church. In many ways, I am a poster pastor for clergy-depression recovery.

Yet, as a relapse is always possible, I must be careful not to forget the life-saving lessons that I have learned. Writing this book is such an act of not forgetting, a continuation of the journaling that I did with those ornery mechanical pencils in the hospital. Now I want to offer these lessons to you. The more I reread this chapter, the more I see the words *I* and *me*. I wasn't brought up to talk so much about myself. That is immodest. But bear with me. I don't know another way to be honest about what I have learned.

On the basis of these last eight years, I believe that I have learned what I need to know to stay healthy. The question is, will I remember

1. Plath, *Bell Jar*, 244.

these lessons when the phone keeps ringing and the calendar is full? At such times of stress, I need to have these lessons somehow pop into my mind, just as the words of psalms that I have memorized will pop into my mind: "Therefore my heart is glad, and my glory rejoiceth: my flesh also shall rest in hope" (Psalm 16:9). For this to happen, I need to keep telling my story.

To say that I live well with depression is another way of saying that I live well with the knowledge that I can be broken. I can still hear in my mind the click of the lock on the door to the psych unit. I don't know where my breaking point is these days, and of course I hope that I will never find out. But if I did want to discover its current coordinates, I would create a witches' brew of stress, starting with basic ingredients like too many phone calls, e-mails, meetings, and people wanting a piece of my time. Then I would add in that the annual meeting is coming up, stewardship is going poorly, and nobody wants to serve as president of the church next year.

Still not enough stress? Still no breaking point? Mix in the toe of a newt and the eye of a bat: There is a major remodeling project in the sanctuary, one that is getting so out of control that the trustees are wondering if the guys they hired (of course at the lowest bid) didn't learn their trade from Laurel and Hardy. Also there is a big wedding in a couple weeks. The building project has to be done, or we'll face the wrath of the bride's mother. Oh, no! The copier just broke down again, and the renewal form for the service contract is still sitting on my desk.

Then to complete the brew, add that I made the rookie mistake of picking up the phone on my way out of the office. I was almost home free, like before I was hospitalized the second time. But I chose to pick up the phone. It's Mr. Big Giver. His wife thinks that no child should have communion until confirmed. He wants to know what I am going to do about her displeasure. He invites me for lunch at his convenience at his club. Really, he has a club.

I used to think at such ultrastressful times that I could just suck it up and tough it out, work as hard as I had to for as long as I had to, while keeping my feelings stuffed down deep. And that I could do this regardless of what it cost me in stress and what toll it took at home. I was wrong. The click of the lock on the psych-unit door was also the sound of me breaking.

So when the symptoms of stress begin to appear (my concentrations fails, I get irritable, my shoulders ache, my anxiety rises), I know that it is time to get help and to get it quickly. I have no choice. I urgently need to move away from work and move toward those who can help me. So I have lunch with Sue, my reliable first line of defense, and we talk things over. She reminds me of all the good that I have done and of all the options that we now have. I e-mail the boys, give them a call, or have a father-son craft-beer night. I call some colleagues and talk things over, discuss all the professional options that I have; sometimes we need to talk face-to-face. I also read my favorite psalms and talk things over with them.

After I have done these basics, the due diligence of recovery, I am calmer and can return to church. With my colleagues I have talked through whom I need to contact and what committees or officers have responsibility for what is going on. So we meet, we talk, and we come up with a plan. They are not my mom, and I don't need to protect them from worry. Confident that things are getting better, I call the bride's mom and invite her out to lunch or coffee. Depending on her tone of voice, I might also invite a female deacon to join us.

Not surprisingly, this imagined witch's-brew scenario of the unfinished church renovations and the upcoming wedding is based on an event from my ministry. The names have been changed to protect the innocent. I end up having lunch one-on-one with the bride's mom. After some justified venting, she becomes quite reasonable and is understanding of the bind that we are in at church. She does make some pointed (and quite accurate) comments about our board of trustees—such as "penny-wise and pound-foolish." Just make sure, she says that we need to be certain that the bathrooms are clean and plaster won't fall on her daughter's head. Seems reasonable to me.

Later that day, the head of the board of trustees calls to say that the copier company will cover the repairs if we re-up our service contract. A couple days later, the head of the stewardship drive calls to apologize: she had just opened a book that a friend had lent her at church and found a couple of completed pledge cards that she had stuck between the pages. On the basis of these new cards, we are doing okay on the pledge drive after all—not great, but okay. She also tells me that after some carefully applied pressure, her husband is willing to serve as vice president. I know him; he will do a good job.

Things are looking up, and it is time for lunch with Mr. Big Giver, who has finally found some spare time for me. I half expect to see mounted pastors' heads on the club walls. But of course the club is all tasteful, subdued, and mahogany. I can feel the power of big bucks surging around the room, very discreet but quite obvious. Thankfully, I had rehearsed this meeting with a colleague. She helped me to realize that as pastor, even as interim pastor, I have lots of power. In a way, I have even more power than a called pastor. I can tell him exactly what I think. I will be gone soon enough. I won't have to deal with him forever.

Besides, I've faced down heinous monsters, and he's just a soft old guy with a fat wallet. He is not half as tough as Dottie on a day when she's feeling mellow. Surely I can cut him a little slack, provided he cuts me some. So we have lunch, little fillet mignons and a glass of wine each from the grapes of joy, which grow in the vineyard opposite the grapes of wrath. "Wine that maketh glad the heart of man" (Psalm 104:15). The familiar words of the psalm make me smile when they pop into my head with the first sip. I am not alone. I am surrounded by a cloud of witnesses.

Over coffee, Mr. Big Giver huffs and puffs a little, but I don't cave in, and soon we are just talking. I learn about his work, how proud he is of what he has accomplished. In some ways, he's like my dad, and I can sure see why guys like him hook my need to please. But he is not my dad. I do not need his approval to survive or be happy in the world. I have outgrown my childish ways.

He tries to impress me with his foreign travels; I counter with stories from trips that Sue and I have taken. Turns out we've both run with the kangaroos in Australia. No kidding! I kind of like the guy. My pastoral side kicks in, and my concern for him is genuine. He is not really that happy. When he finally gets around to his wife, he tells me about her conservative background and her belief that communion is something children earn through confirmation.

We talk theology and find some common ground. We develop a plan in which his wife will work with the Christian education committee to prepare our church's children to receive communion, whatever their age. We have made a deal. I am sure that it wasn't the only deal made over coffee in that place that day, though it may have been the only one that did not involve serious money, just self-respect.

I have a little bust of Robert E. Lee in the glass-fronted secretary at home. I got it somewhere when I was a child, probably on a trip to Williamsburg, Virginia, with my folks. Robert E. Lee was all about honor. He would have been proud of how I behaved that day.

After lunch my host doesn't pick up the check because a check never appears. I would love to belong to such a club! (Of course, they also didn't give us a check with Chef's Choice at the hospital either.) Driving home, I can feel the tension ebb out of my shoulders. I had been appropriately honest, but of course I did not tell him that the Christian education committee had been talking about such a communion class for some time and had been casting around for somebody to teach it—with no takers. Mr. Big Giver has his cards to play, and I have mine. I am a professional. Like Sisyphus, I smile.

Some things go poorly; others go well. Any day can be Christmas. Lean toward the light. Get help crossing the rocky ground. Don't try to control other people; they did not sign up to play roles in scripts that you wrote. If you want some slack, cut other people some slack. Beware of illogical thinking in all its forms; it will break your heart. You can't meet everybody's expectations. Do your job. Don't do other people's jobs. Be good to yourself. Don't miss opportunities for pleasure. Make sure that your pants are zipped up before you leave home. Such is my essential wisdom for living well with depression.

This wisdom offers tactics for maintaining one's inner balance in times of stress. Again as Amma Syncletica said so long ago, "Lack of proportion always corrupts."[2] You can find examples in any newspaper of the destructive results of lack of proportion. You can also find them in many great movies. *All about Eve*, starring Bette Davis at the height of her power as an actress, is a cautionary tale of how losing your inner balance and sense of proportion can turn a good thing into evil.

In the movie, Margot Channing (Bette Davis) is honest about what aging means to her as a woman and as an actress. One admires her for her courage in acknowledging the truth as she sees it. But she becomes obsessed by her age and its perceived impact on her career and personal life. As the signs of aging appear, she believes that all the good roles will disappear. (Sadly, there may be some truth in this.) But a source of far more pain for Margot is her belief that her boyfriend cannot really love an older woman like herself. Nothing in his behavior supports this fear. It is her obsession and anxiety, not her age, that almost drives him away from her for good.

Margot is not the only one who can act so self-destructively. When I lose inner balance and sense of proportion, my honesty about my motives and actual accomplishments (a good thing) morphs into fierce self-criticism (a bad thing). It becomes a monster that makes no allowances

2. Quoted in Norris, *Dakota*, 213.

and accepts no forgiveness. It is as destructive to me as Margot's anxiety is for her. Most of the time, I can keep a healthy balance between honest self-criticism and honest self-satisfaction. But when these two feelings get out of balance, my behavior becomes as self-destructive and as self-defeating as Margot's.

The balance between honesty and self-criticism isn't the only inner balancing act that I need to attend to: I take responsibility (a good thing). I have a tendency to take too much responsibility, including responsibility that belongs to other people (a bad thing). I have a strong work ethic (a good thing). I tend to overperform (not so good). I really care about people and want to make people happy (a good thing). I can be a people pleaser (a bad thing). I have a good sense of humor that gives me perspective (a good thing). I can use humor to avoid facing reality (a bad thing). I care about the quality of my work (a good thing). I am a perfectionist (a bad and unhealthy thing).

I also know that I am a work in progress and always will be. Though I crave reality, there is so much about myself, the world, and the people in it that baffles me. And my theology, which is supposed to help me understand, just refuses to stay put. Whenever I get into such a state, I call to mind some lines from *The Big Lebowski*, directed by Joel Coen, a native of St. Louis Park, Minnesota, my hometown for the last thirty-five years. In the movie, The Dude (Jeff Bridges—no relation to Dude in *Rio Bravo*) explains the hazards of dealing with complicated intellectual issues:

> This is a very complicated case, Maude. You know, a lotta ins, a lotta outs, a lotta what-have-yous. And, um, a lotta strands to keep in my head, man. Lotta strands in old Duder's head. Fortunately, I'm adhering to a pretty strict, uh, drug regimen to keep my mind, you know, um, limber.[3]

I don't think that the old Duder's drug regimen involved antidepressants. That being said, like him I've got lots of strands in my head—"a lotta ins, a lotta outs, a lotta what-have-yous." Some of these strands I can untangle; some I can weave into something good. But some are just tangled up in a big ball. And if I spend all my time up in my head trying to untangle them, they will use up all my time, and I will accomplish nothing.

When the case gets too complicated for the Dude, and the strands get too many, he gets out of his head and back to reality by going to his

3. *The Big Lebowski*, DVD, dir. Coen.

holy place—not to Tiffany's and certainly not to Rock Ridge or a church, but to a bowling alley. Good for the Dude! When the same happens to me, I go for a walk, read Psalm 40, perhaps visit somebody at a nursing home, or maybe head to my favorite coffeehouse, not to hide but to read the *New York Times* and enjoy the pleasure of a scone and, if I get lucky, maybe a song. Holy places are everywhere.

Here's one more essential point about living well with depression: you must have an emergency plan B. Early on in my recovery, when stress was rising and my means of coping were failing, my plan B was an emergency call to my therapist or psychiatrist. If you are recovering from depression and serious symptoms return, I urge you to do the same. If you don't have a psychiatrist, call somebody. If there isn't anybody, 911 will do.

For the last several years, emergency calls to my psychiatrist have not been necessary. I think that this is partly because I now have so many people in my life who know what happened to me. Depending on what's going on, I can always call one of them, and frequently I do. Also something odd has happened over time: my recovery has strengthened itself, it has become self-sustaining. You spiral down; you spiral up. These days I expect to be happy. Even when I am unhappy, I know that the unhappiness won't last. A positive mental attitude works for golfers and quarterbacks. Why should it not work for preachers? Why should it not work for all of us who are recovering from depression?

I have known for a long time now what it's like to feel good. Feeling good is my "new normal," my default setting. I suspect that this is what the various antidepressant medications aim for. For several years 90 milligrams of Cymbalta helped secure my mood. Then, with much care, my psychiatrist and I decreased my dosage—never in winter—so that now I no longer take antidepressants. Yes, this does feel like a victory, but in a heartbeat I would restart antidepressants if my mood slipped downhill. I expect to feel good, and that makes all the difference.

So when the stress rises and depression beckons to me, I stand a little straighter, take a deep breath, and say, "Screw you. You've done your worst to me, and here I am, standing upright on solid ground with my friends gathered around me. You tell me I've made a mistake. I say, so what! Do you think I'm God? Well, I don't. Besides, making mistakes is just the flip side of having successes. At least I have the courage to do something. You know what? I'm busy, and I don't have room for you in my life anymore. So get out of my head. I've got work to do and fun to have." Exit depression—at least for a while.

Once I had my life taken out of my hands. Now I have taken it back again. To do this, I have had to grow up and become myself, an adult child of God with the courage to act honestly to meet my own needs. From the outside, these thoughts may sound like an excerpt clipped from a middle-brow advice column. But from the inside, from inside my life, they sustain my self-respect.

And in my recovery I have learned how hydra-headed an attack on one's self-respect can be. A good example comes from Saul Bellow's novel *The Adventures of Augie March*. Augie is offered the opportunity to work in a fancy store, if he has the right look. But there is a price in indignity to be paid.

> He had me strip my jacket so he could see my shoulders and my fanny, so that I was just about to tell him what he could do with his job when he said I was built right for his purpose, and my vanity was more influential than my self-respect. He then said to me, "I want to put you in my saddle shop—riding habits, boots, dude-ranch stuff, fancy articles. I'll pay twenty bucks a week while you're learning, and when you're broken in I'll pay you twenty-five plus commission."
>
> Naturally I took the job. I'd be earning more money than Simon.[4]

In taking the job, both Augie's vanity and his ongoing competition with his brother Simon trump his self-respect. Earning more than his brother Simon will be a feast for Augie's needy ego. His story is a cautionary tale for me. People with self-respect, people like me, are sufficiently sure of their value so that they don't need to pump up their egos with vanity or stroke them with petty success.

What about pumping up your ego by preaching? Isn't this a threat to one's self-respect? Isn't preaching an exercise in vanity? Isn't a pulpit robe with those liturgically correct colored stoles simply a disguise for egotism? Consider in this regard some lines from the film *Three Colors: Red* by Krzysztof Kiéslowski. I first came across them in a movie review by Anthony Lane. Lane describes what happens toward the end of the movie. A retired judge, played by Jean-Louis Trintignant, is speaking.

---

4. Bellow, *Augie March*, 140.

> ". . . deciding what is true and what isn't now seems to me—"
> He stops, searching for the proper phrase, and finds it: "a lack
> of modesty."[5]

I know exactly what this feels like and the self-doubt that it engenders: Who do I think I am? How can I stand up there Sunday after Sunday acting like I have some insight into deep truths, or even shallow truths for that matter? And yet I keep plugging along as a minister, preaching the gospel as best I can. Maybe I'm like Rocky (Sylvester Stallone), the star of the eponymous movies, when his girlfriend Adrian (Talia Shire) asks, "Why do you want to fight?"

"Because I can't sing or dance."[6]

Me neither. So I keep preaching.

In fact, I enjoy being a minister, and I am too wise a person to despise pleasure. Moreover I'm pretty good at ministry. People tell me so, and I'm learning not to disqualify the positive. Looking back, I even did good ministry on the psych unit. Being open about what I did for a living gained me the respect of Dottie and other patients on the unit. To be honest, it wasn't as if I was doing something brave; it was just that when people asked me what I did, I told them. Maybe I lacked the energy to make something up. But I do believe that because I was open, people were more open with me, and that's good ministry.

I also served the sacrament of the cup of Christ on the unit. One day during my first hospitalization while I was sitting in the common room reading, a particularly fragile young woman dropped a glass of water as she stumbled against a chair. Finding some paper towels and cleaning up the mess seemed beyond her. I got some towels and got down on my knees and helped her wipe up the mess. She thanked me, and I went over to the sink and got her another glass of water. When I handed it to her, I had a flash memory of handing the cup to a parishioner at communion. Now I think about her on Communion Sundays at church.

Moving from the psych unit to the pulpit is a wonderful way to avoid becoming inflated about who you are when you preach. This woman I served communion to, as well as Dottie and the others on the unit who respected me as a minister, are among the cloud of witnesses I keep faith with on Sunday mornings. Like them, like the folks in the pews, I am seeking something that is life-giving now and something that will give

---

5. Lane, *Nobody's Perfect*, 91.
6. *Rocky*, DVD, dir. Avildsen.

me hope in the future. I have some Scriptures to share about this. They have helped me; I pray that they will help you. It's not egotism. It's the best that I have to offer. After all, I can't sing or dance.

My work as an interim pastor has helped reinforce my recovery. As an interim (a "temp," as I was called in one church—"Need help? Call Bob, the temp. Bob can do it."), I have a particular job to do. Either I am helping church members grieve over the pastor who has left, or I am helping them to get ready for the pastor who is coming. These are processes that can involve considerable mixed feelings. Either way, it's not about me. At one time I erased the boundaries between my life and the church; that is death for a professional. Being an effective interim is all about knowing where these boundaries lie. It's on-the-job mental-health training, and I'm good at it.

A friend of mine, a seasoned interim, says that he always makes it a point to start screwing up a couple weeks before the new pastor arrives. On his last couple Sundays he pulls out his worst sermons and preaches them with studied dullness. Given that he's not the world's most dynamic guy, this is probably not all that hard for him. Still, he does have a point that hits home to me. If I succumb to my tendency to overdo and over-perform as an interim pastor, trying at whatever the cost never to make a mistake, I'm setting the bar too high for the next person.

In other words, doing the best job I can as an interim means performing at a normal, sustainable level, letting the mistakes come where they may. What a corrective for a perfectionist! If you do too much and do it too well, you've failed in the task of helping the church to set reasonable long-term expectations for the new pastor.

You can learn a lot by being a temp. Good interims are valuable professionals, worth their weight in gold-embossed Bibles. So if you need some help, why not call old Bob? He is a temp with a difference. I am serious here. As an interim, I'm always looking for that next job, and I might be unemployed when you read this. Talk about learning how to live with uncertainty! Try interim ministry. It will teach you that you are not in control. And don't forget to make that call to good old Bob.

I did something recently that I have never done in my forty plus years of ordained ministry: I bought a black shirt with a clerical collar. True, I had borrowed one once from a colleague to wear while I was picketing with Susan at her hospital on behalf of her nurses' union. Fight the powers that be! And it was great. Several of the perky young female nurses came up to me and asked, "Can I have my picture taken with you, Father?"

"Of course you can, my dear." Oh yes, ministry can be a great line of work.

The clerical shirt I bought is a jet-black, short-sleeved affair, manufactured by the Friar Tuck Company. I'm not kidding. Actually, I almost bought a purple one, which would have looked great at the gay-pride parade. But the salesman asked, "Are we a bishop, sir?" I swear that his tone of voice, condescending but caring, was exactly the same as the Tiffany salesman who waited on Holly and Paul in the movie.

My initial reason for buying the clergy shirt was similar to why I borrowed one once before: it was a political action. In this case, a group of us was going to a meeting of the county board of supervisors, and I knew that I would make more of an impact in a clerical shirt. Actually, when I spoke to the board, it seemed to me that the shirt was working. They all made eye contact and looked appropriately deferential. Score one for Friar Tuck.

Even better and more telling about my recovery is what happened next. Rather than put my clerical shirt away until the next demonstration, I wore it to church the next Sunday. I had never worn a clergy shirt to church before in my life. You can imagine my disappointment when most people failed to notice anything different about me. Then again, I was a temp; I'd only been there for six months or so. One guy did notice it and remarked, "Well, I guess we're in for it today."

Actually they were in for it. I used the shirt as a sermon illustration of self-acceptance, coming to terms with who you are and what you do. I talked about the fact that I had never worn a clergy shirt before in church, let alone in the pulpit, and described how I felt about wearing the shirt. It was a good sermon in that it was all true. I used Psalm 40 as the text, and the message was something like my journey from the pit of depression to being in the pulpit wearing my spiffy Friar Tuck clergy shirt.

As you can see, most days I'm living well with depression, remembering what I have learned, and keeping the demands of my profession in balance with my limits—even doing it with some grace and humor. True, I haven't worn my clergy shirt since that Sunday, but I know I'll wear it again when I preach. I'm just looking for the right text or occasion. I look good in it. This isn't vanity; it's positive feedback I receive that I do not disqualify. And, son of my dad to the end, I'm going to get my money's worth out of the shirt.

CHAPTER 12

From Psych Unit to Pulpit

BACK IN THE DAY, when England had ecclesiastical as well as secular courts, access to this more merciful judicial system was a great benefit for clergy. Over time this benefit was extended to all who were literate, both lay and clergy. Even better, to be considered literate, one didn't really have to be able to read and write, just able to recite. Psalm 51 became the standard text for recitation. Memorize Psalm 51 and you would escape the potential capital punishment of the secular court. Hence Psalm 51 became known as the "neck verse," as it could literally save one's neck. In 1581 it saved the neck of the dramatist Ben Jonson.

Psalm 51 is one of the "neck verses" in my recovery from depression. I have memorized much of it, as I have a number of psalms, not because I am anticipating a return to old ways of jurisprudence but because I like knowing things by heart. I can feed on them there. They are there when I need them. If there are verses in a psalm that don't help me, I just don't memorize them. Earlier today I was working on an order of service for the coming Sunday. While paging through the hymnal, the phrase "singing a new song" from Psalm 40 kept coming back to me. Living well with depression is about "singing a new song." It is about practicing each day what one has learned in order to avoid a relapse.

The phrase "singing a new song" also brings a smile to my face because of a church story from my postdepression life. I was called out at one of the small churches that I served as an interim because I wasn't singing any songs at all—new or used. A woman at this church, who had faced many troubles in her own life, caught me mouthing the words of the opening hymn, while I was covertly using the hymn time to read over my sermon.

How did I expect her to sing, she asked, if I don't sing the hymns myself? If I wanted them to sing alone, then I should at least stop picking hymns that nobody knows. Now, in honor of her, I sing all the hymns lustily, right there in church in front of everybody. I also make sure that the microphone is turned off. Singing, however lustily, ought not to be amplified when it is severely off key. Nevertheless, once you put your mind to it, singing is easy and fun. Maybe it is wishful thinking, but I think that I am improving as a hymn crooner.

I wish that my spiritual recovery could always be as easy as singing hymns. Just as hymn singing is easier when I'm part of a wider congregation, so recovery is strengthened when I am part of a community that cares about me. This makes it easy for me to remember that there is a great cloud of witnesses, saints above and folks in various churches here below, who are cheering me on. When I stay close to people (close to the psalmists from long ago and close to my parishioners right now), my faith feels strong and my recovery feels secure.

But when I start doing theology, moving from the world of people to the world inside my head, my recovery becomes hard work. Needing faith but also needing to be truthful about my doubt, I struggle with being honest about what I really believe. I know that I can lose myself and my faith in this struggle. It is a balancing act that Amma Syncletica would understand. In my spiritual recovery, I need to hold my doubt and faith together. I am a soulmate of the distraught father who cried out to Jesus, "Lord, I believe; help thou mine unbelief" (Mark 9:24b). I am a soulmate of Jesus on the cross, who cried out to his Father the words from Psalm 22, "My God, my God, why hast thou forsaken me?" (Matthew 27:46b).

I have found a way to faith, while being honest about my unbelief. I have undergone spiritual recovery. But why should you listen to me? After all, for many people, depression still carries a stigma. For a minister this stigma can be a particular problem.

If I am a person of faith, which seems like the kind of thing a minister should be, how did I get so depressed? It's a pretty punk minister who doesn't even have enough faith to keep himself out of the loony bin. Whatever faith this guy's got, I want the other kind.

Actually, I have become a much better minister and a more faithful Christian because of my time in the loony bin, but I can't deny the accusation that my being depressed reflects on my faith. To deal with this allegation and with my doubt, you need to know a little more about how I got into my line of work in the first place.

When I was growing up in Richmond, Virginia, I used to sit in church with the starched collar of my too-small white shirt cutting into my sunburned neck and listen to the preacher preach. He impressed me by his ability to explain Scriptures and by the big words he used. He sounded like Walter Cronkite in a pulpit robe. I had learned some of these words and something about how to think clearly from reading a lot in school, which I did so that I could make good grades and please my dad. But over time, the reading became a joy in itself. I fell in love with learning, whether I found it in a book or in a sermon.

When it came time for confirmation, I wore out the confirmation manual on church history and theology. I am still this way. Learning new things gives me pleasure; new learning is like French toast and crispy bacon for the mind. And of course to make my dad proud, I studied hard for the written confirmation exam. I was the first student ever to get 100 percent on the multiple-choice part of the exam. If you have doubts about this, I suspect that you can go to the archives of St. John's United Church of Christ in Richmond, Virginia, and look it up.

The pastor who confirmed me asked me to consider ordained ministry as a career choice. I nodded my head, but in my heart I knew that I would do that only after I had finished my two terms as president of the United States. And while I was president, I would work for social justice. Confirmation had changed me. It was the first time I really thought about what it means to say Jesus loves all people: red and yellow, black and white. I started doing theology: if Jesus loves all people, why were there no black people in my church, even though there are plenty of them right down the street? I had a long road to travel before I became an ordained minister, but I was on my way.

Ultimately this road, the proverbial long and winding one, led me from Richmond to pulpits here in the heartland, thanks to my Minnesota spouse. For many years my interest in theology and philosophy, my desire to make the world a better place for all God's people, and the good feeling I got from helping people sustained me and gave me joy in my pastoral work, at least enough joy to keep me going. And to be completely honest, like most Southerners, I love to talk. Now I was getting paid to talk on a regular basis. It was a sweet deal.

Fine. But when I was falling into the pit of depression, I needed something to break the fall, something more spiritually solid than theological speculation, good intentions, a gift of gab, and the satisfaction found in making people happy. I did not know I needed this until I fell into my depression. Until then, I did not feel that I was faking anything. This is my faith story, and I am not ashamed to tell it. Writing this, telling my story as clearly as I can, I have already come a long way in exorcising for myself whatever stigma is attached to being a very depressed man of God.

As you know, I found the spiritual strength that I needed for recovery in the Psalms. More exactly, I found it first of all in the faith of those who wrote the Psalms. I can put it this way: in my spiritual recovery, I have found that there is a rock that supports my faith. But it's a borrowed rock, kind of a sedimentary rock composed in good measure of the faith of others.

I have found my rock, but my doubts and questions persist, as they did for the father who sought help for his unbelief, as they did for Jesus, and also as they did for a character in the movie *Hannah and Her Sisters*, directed by Woody Allen. In the movie, Mickey (Allen) challenges his father about the existence of all the evil in the world. What about the Nazis, for example? Why did God permit such a thing? His dad answers, "How the hell do I know why there were Nazis! I don't even know how a can opener works."[1]

Like Mickey's dad, I don't know how a can opener works, especially the industrial-sized can openers one finds in church kitchens. I certainly don't know why there were Nazis. God's answer to Job about why the innocent suffer makes me a better person every time I read it, less lost in my head and more committed to doing justice in the world. But having read the passage, been touched by it yet again, I still want to ask God, "So, Mr. God Almighty, why exactly do the innocent suffer?"

I want to cut myself as much slack as possible here, not to lose my balance as Margot did in *All about Eve*. Maybe my doubting is simply genetic. Hence it is not my fault. There is nothing I can do about it, a nice escape for me. In Chekov's short story "On the Road," Liharev, a traveler and dreamer, says:

> The way I look at it is that faith is a faculty of the spirit. It is just the same as a talent, one must be born with it. So far as I can judge by myself, by the people I have seen in my time, and by all that is done around us, this faculty is present in Russians in its highest degree.[2]

1. *Hannah and Her Sisters*, DVD, dir. Allen.
2. Chekov, *Chorus Girl*, 210.

Well, I am not a Russian, so what do you expect? I lack the faculty. It's hard for me to say that I believe something without proof, a legacy of all the philosophy classes that I took in college and graduate school before I started seminary. I wish that I could just say that I believe in God and leave it at that. But I lack the faculty of the spirit.

In *Amazing Grace: A Vocabulary of Faith*, Kathleen Norris describes an article she read about an argument between a seminary student, who seems a lot like me, and an Orthodox theologian. The seminarian could not affirm certain tenets of the creed. The article does not specify which ones. He and the theologian argue back and forth for a while. The seminarian insists that he cannot say a creed that he does not fully believe in. Norris describes the priest's retort.

> "It's not your creed, it's our creed," meaning the Creed of the entire Christian church. I can picture the theologian shrugging, as only the Orthodox can shrug, carrying so lightly the thousand-plus years of their liturgical tradition: "Eventually it may come to you," he told the student. "For some, it takes longer than for others."[3]

Of course, I also have had lots of trouble with the creeds. The virgin birth? Give me a break. I'm still struggling with "I believe." Hell? Heaven?" Oh, please! But I have mellowed, maybe actually gotten a little wiser spiritually: I have learned how to say the Apostles' Creed. Indeed I have learned to say it much in the spirit of the Orthodox priest in the story. I learned how to say it in the same little church where I was chided for not singing.

Though a United Church of Christ church, this church uses a Methodist hymnal that has the Apostles' Creed as part of the communion liturgy. When the Methodist church in town closed, some of its members came to the UCC church and brought a big box of hymnals with them. These hymnals were in a lot better condition than the tattered UCC ones, so it was easy for these folks to decide which hymnals to keep. Many of these folks are retired small farmers who have lived through the death of their way of life. They have survived in good measure by being pragmatic. They don't throw out perfectly good hymnals just because they have *Methodist* on the cover.

It was a privilege to lead such a congregation in worship. When I came to the Apostles' Creed in the communion liturgy, it was easy to say

3. Norris, *Amazing Grace*, 65.

the Creed along with the people. Besides, I'd memorized it in confirmation, and the words came back from fifty or so years ago. It was as if, in worship at this church with these folks, doubt did not apply. I trusted these people; I trusted their church; and I trusted their Creed. I don't believe much of the Creed literally, but I passionately believe in saying all of it together with the people of God. Besides, if I say it enough, it may come to me.

Here are two brief points: First, saying the Apostles' Creed felt good, and I have come to trust the rightness of this feeling. It is the kind of good feeling that has become the default emotional setting for me in my recovery. Second, someday I might get to heaven and some woman might come up to me and say, "Hey, Bob, what's up? I'm the Virgin Mary that you've been hearing so much about. I believe in you, Bob. Why don't you believe in me?" Who knows? It could happen. Really, who knows? Doubt keeps one's options open.

Barbara Brown Taylor in *The Preaching Life* offers another example of how one can borrow the faith of others. In commenting on a conversation with someone for whom credo "sticks in her mind like a splinter,"[4] Taylor writes:

> All I could give her was what I give myself—the reassurance that the creed is said in the plural, not the singular. When I say, "We believe . . ." I count on that to cover what I cannot believe on my own right now. When my faith limps, I lean on the faith of the church, letting "our" faith suffice until "mine" returns.[5]

Later in the same book, she says that she does not know anyone who believes all the time. She describes belief as being like a rope bridge.

> It is not a well-fluffed nest, or a well-defended castle high on a hill. It is more like a rope bridge over a scenic gorge, sturdy but swinging back and forth, with plenty of light and plenty of air but precious little to hang on to except stories you have heard: that it is the best and only way across, that it is possible, that it will bear your weight.[6]

Taylor's last image, of faith as a bridge, feels quite a bit safer than Søren Kierkegaard's "leap" or "leap on faith."[7] The better-known phrase,

---

4. Taylor, *Preaching Life*, 71.

5. Ibid.

6. Ibid., 93.

7. Kierkegaard, *Purity of Heart*, 16.

"leap of faith," is something ministers do when we ask for a raise. It is not a kierkegaardian term. I learned this at the church I recently served in as an interim, in Northfield, Minnesota, the home of St. Olaf College, which is in turn home to the Howard and Edna Hong Kierkegaard Library. I attended a Kierkegaard conference there led by a Dane who was semifluent in English. We have Kierkegaard scholars in my congregation. So far, none have leapt noticeably during a service.

If we trust the faith of others at the places where our own faith is weak, as I trust the authors of the psalms of lament and wise parishioners, then their faith can be a bridge from us to God. We don't have to leap; we just trust the bridge that they give us. Indeed much has been written in recent years (recent years include all the years since I left seminary) about faith as trust. Faith understood as trust underlies what has come to be known as progressive theology, associated with theologians like Marcus Borg.

In *Speaking Christian: Why Christian Words Have Lost Their Meaning and Power—And How They Can Be Restored*, Borg relates the origin of *faith*, *belief*, and related words. He writes that before the year 1600, the verb *believe* was always followed by the name of a person, not by a statement. Borg says that *believe* comes from an Old German word that means "to hold dear." It is similar to our word *beloved*.[8] He goes on to say:

> Thus until the 1600s, to *believe in* God and Jesus meant to *belove* God and Jesus. Think of the difference this makes. To believe in God does not mean *believing that* a set of statements about God are true, but to *belove* God. To believe in Jesus does not mean to *believe that* a set of statements about him are true, but to *belove* Jesus.[9]

In a similar manner Borg goes back to the original meaning of *faith*, defined as "fidelity and trust." He writes:

> Think of how different faith as fidelity and trust, as *fidelitas* and *fiducia*, is from faith as believing a set of statements to be true.[10]

This understanding of *belief* as loving and *faith* as trusting is of great help to me in my struggle to be honest with my doubts. I do have a faculty for loving and a faculty for trusting. I love the church; I love the people;

8. Ibid., 118.

9. Ibid., 119.

10. Ibid., 122.

I love being a minister to the people. I trust in the faith of others, and I trust the God that they trust in.

But I cannot go all the way with Borg. I still want faith as a set of statements, as in the Apostles' Creed. I am too much of a philosopher to let go of propositions. I want to pin faith down. But I want lots of things that I will never get. So, as Sean Connery's character says in *The Untouchables*, "Here endeth the lesson."[11]

In the meantime, I trust in God so much that I can cease being a "functional atheist," to use Parker Palmer's phrase, and I can turn over to God that which is beyond my control. I don't think one can recover spiritually without learning how to do this. This is also the spiritual wisdom of Alcoholics Anonymous. In some form or other, I suspect that half the sermons that I preach these days have "surrender," "turn it over," or some form of the "Serenity Prayer" as a theme.

I look for images and metaphors that are true to belief and faith, which I understand as love and trust. In the preface to *Encountering God: A Spiritual Journey from Bozeman to Banaras*, Diana Eck uses images to give the road map that I am trying to follow.

> This is a book about faith and the challenge religious diversity poses to people of faith in every religious tradition. It is a book that begins with the premise that our religious traditions are more like rivers than monuments. They are not static and they are not over. They are still rolling—with forks and confluences, rapids and waterfalls. Where those rivers of faith flow depends upon who we are and who we become. . . . It is a book about how my encounters with people of other faiths have challenged, changed, and deepened my own.[12]

This is true for my faith. Built on a rock, the sedimentary rock of faith borrowed from others, my faith also flows like a river. Not any one metaphor captures all the truth of it. My faith has its "forks and confluences, rapids and waterfalls"; but it keeps flowing over, around, and through these obstructions. And like a river that draws from hidden springs, great lakes, or deep snows, so my faith arises from the inexhaustible source of a communities' experience of God, "the Fount of Every Blessing."

I've mentioned that friends have commented on how my sermons have changed since I started getting well. These days my faith and my

11. *The Untouchables*, DVD, dir. De Palma.
12. Eck, *Encountering God*, ix.

sermons flow together—not always smoothly, but they keep flowing. And I don't always feel that I am in control. (Though if I want to say "keep on trucking" in a sermon, no matter how well the words are flowing, I do seek careful control of these three words, especially *trucking.*)

Like Diana Eck, I have encountered people of other faiths. Though these include Jews, Buddhists, and Muslims, mostly they are people with other versions of Christian faith, folks who've built their faith on other rocks. Honestly, for a few of them, faith has a self-righteousness and judgmental certainty that does not help me. In fact, I hate it. My faith just flows on around them.

However, the faith of most people I encounter feeds into my own, causing it to flow in new and interesting directions. I am a great observer these days of the first commandment. Since I am not God and don't have all the truth, my faith naturally changes course when I encounter the truth of another faith. My ability to let this happen is another sign of my spiritual healing.

As my river of faith rolls along, I come upon new realities in the world and in my own life. In *The Psalms and the Life of Faith*, Walter Brueggemann sets this experience of newness in theological perspective:

> Those who have entered deeply into "the pit" may presume that is the permanent situation, when, in fact, life has moved on and their circumstances have been transformed toward newness. In such times, the songs of celebration may lead the person or community to embrace the context of newness in which they live.
>
> . . . In dramatic and dynamic ways, the songs can also function to evoke and form new realities that did not exist until, or apart from, the actual singing of the song.[13]

Brueggemann could be responding here to the opening of my beloved Psalm 40.

> I waited patiently for the LORD; and he inclined unto me, and heard my cry.
> He brought me up also out of an horrible pit, out of the miry clay, and set my feet upon a rock, and established my goings.
> And he hath put a new song in my mouth, even praise unto our God: many shall see it, and fear, and shall trust in the LORD.

13. Brueggemann, *Message of the Psalms*, 28.

> Blessed is that man that maketh the LORD his trust, and re-
> specteth not the proud, nor such as turn aside to lies. (Psalm
> 40:1–4)

The quote and the psalm are about movement as opposed to stasis; they are about transformation and "new realities" as opposed to the pit and a "permanent situation." Such is the river of my faith. At the same time, my faith is a rock under my feet: "set my feet upon a rock and established my goings." This is one of my "new realities."

As the psalm shows, both metaphors are accurate. My faith as a rock does not allow me to "turn aside to lies," which happens when I listen to my fears or to those who would diminish my God-given self-respect. I don't need to contort myself and try to live a lie to please somebody. God knows that I am not perfect, but I am still God's child.

To say that my faith is a river is the same as saying that I have options in my life. Options can be scary; but they are also exhilarating, an expression of what it is to be truly alive. In the classic movie *The African Queen*, Charles Allnut (Humphrey Bogart), the profane, hard-drinking captain of the *African Queen*, is shamed by Rose Sayer (Katherine Hepburn), the sister of an extremely proper and censorious missionary, into taking off down a mighty river to pursue her crazy idea of using his little steamboat to somehow sink a huge German gunboat on Lake Victoria. Allnut hopes that a trip over some serious rapids will convince her that her idea is, in fact, crazy. After going through the rapids he asks her:

> Charlie Allnut: How'd you like it?
> Rose Sayer: Like it?
> Charlie Allnut: White-water rapids!
> Rose Sayer: I never dreamed . . .
> Charlie Allnut: I don't blame you for being scared—not a bit.
>   Nobody with good sense ain't scared of white water.
> Rose Sayer: I never dreamed that any mere physical experience
>   could be so stimulating![14]

By the end of the movie, Rose has learned a lot more about how physical experiences can be stimulating, and Allnut has learned about self-respect. For me, the rapids are like choices—scary but life giving. Being "transformed toward newness" is risky. Change is hard. But as we say in interim ministry, there is no growth without change. You have to ride

---

14. *The African Queen*, DVD, dir. Huston.

the rapids to get down the river. As for Rose, so for a church: knowing you're not in control, actually trusting in God, is spiritually exhilarating.

I've focused on the metaphors of rock and river to express my faith in spiritual recovery. Lots of other metaphors would also work: "path," "refuge," "green pastures," "tree planted by rivers of water," "mighty fortress," "under thy wings," "sanctuary," "way," and so on. All these metaphors live for me. They capture part of the truth of my unique experience of God, often mediated as it is through the faith of others.

In discussing my faith in terms of metaphors drawn from Scripture, I am indebted to William Brown. In *Seeing the Psalms: A Theology of Metaphor*, Brown makes a point similar to the points made by Borg and other progressive Christian writers, but he makes it in terms of one's use of images and metaphors.

> Scripture is not so much a source of propositions, much less a series of creeds or doctrines, as "a vast collection of interwoven images." Moreover, the imaginative act is not confined to the construction of singular, concrete images. An image is invariably supported by a constellation of images that help to establish an evocative setting or orienting framework.[15]

Though I have had to search for faith, these days hope just seems to keep bubbling up inside of me. Eight years into my recovery, I still stretch out in bed before going to sleep and smile. I am sure that sleep will come quickly, and I am amazed that I'm not dreading the morning. "I laid me down and slept; I awakened; because the LORD sustained me" (Psalm 3:5). And not only do I awake, I awake with hope that it will be another good day.

When it comes to faith, I am a borrower. But when it comes to hope, I am a lender. Others can cover their despair with my hope. My experience of finding hope in my recovery brings me once again to words of the Psalms.

> "Why art thou cast down, O my soul? And why art thou disquieted within me? hope thou in God: for I shall yet praise him, who is the health of my countenance, and my God. (Psalm 42:11; see also Psalms 42:5 and 43:5)

Hope is a major theme of the movie *The Shawshank Redemption*. Andy Durfresne (Tim Robbins) is in Shawshank Prison for murdering

---

15. Brown, *Seeing the Psalms*, 11.

his wife, a crime that he did not commit. He makes friends with Red (Morgan Freeman), who is a long-term inmate and a survivor. As their friendship grows, Andy opens his heart to Red.

> Andy: . . . there are places in this world that aren't made out of stone. That there's something inside . . . that they can't get to, that they can't touch. That's yours.
> Red: What're you talking about?
> Andy: Hope.
> Red: Let me tell you something, my friend. Hope is a dangerous thing. Hope can drive a man insane.[16]

Red is a wise man: he knows how to survive in prison. But Andy turns out to be a wiser man: he knows how to escape from prison. He does this literally at the climax of the movie. But by keeping hope alive, he actually freed his spirit from prison much earlier than he freed his body.

In *The Prophetic Imagination*, Walter Brueggemann writes about hope:

> It is the task of the prophet to bring to expression the new realities against the more visible ones of the old order. Energizing is closely linked to hope. We are energized not by that which we already possess but by that which is promised and about to be given.[17]

I'm not saying that Andy is such a prophet, but I wouldn't be surprised if he were. His hope kept him energized and working toward a new reality, a new life outside prison, and he achieved his goal. Not only that: in the end he was able to cover Red's doubt with his hope, so Red also found a new life outside of Shawshank. Like me, Andy has hope to share.

Andrew Solomon writes:

> In good spirits, some love themselves and some love others and some love work and some love God: any of these passions can furnish that vital sense of purpose that is the opposite of depression.[18]

I love them all. As various images reveal and sustain my faith, so these various loves sustain and enliven my hope. They all give me another

16. *The Shawshank Redemption*, Blu-ray, dir. Darabont.

17. Brueggemann, *Prophetic Imagination*, 14.

18. Solomon, *Noonday Demon*, 15.

reason to get up in the morning; they all show me that there is a purpose for living. Like Andy Durfresne, I am energized by hope.

I once heard Parker Palmer give a talk at the Westminster Town Hall Forum in Minneapolis. The place was packed, a sign of hope in its own right. Palmer spoke about his new book, *Habits of the Heart*. Someone in the audience asked him, given all the problems in our political system, particularly the corrupting role of big money, how he felt about the future of our democracy. He answered, and I wrote it down as he spoke, "I always put my money on hope. If for no other reason, then it gives me something to do."[19]

I also put my money down on hope. This is my hearty decision. I don't have unlimited time to wait for the evidence to come in. I don't want to be like those two old monks who procrastinated until they had wasted their lives. And like The Dude, I haven't got all day to sit around trying to untangle all the strands that are in my head. So I have to do the best I can with what I know now, make my choices, and ride whatever rapids the river leads me to. At least I'm trucking along.

There a great line in the classic movie *The Apartment* that brings home how I live now. Fran Kubelik (Shirley MacLane) has had tough luck with men. As she says at one point, "When you're in love with a married man, you shouldn't wear mascara."[20] At another point, J. J. Baxter (Jack Lemon) tells her that the mirror on her compact is cracked. Fran answers, "Yes, I know. I like it that way. Makes me look the way I feel."[21] Later in the movie J. J. saves Miss Kubelik from a suicide attempt. Finally things calm down, and they are playing gin rummy. Laying his cards right on the table, J. J. tells Miss Kubelik that he loves her. She seems not to have heard.

> J. J. Baxter: You hear what I said, Miss Kubelik? I absolutely adore you?
> Fran Kubelik: Shut up and deal.[22]

That's it. When she says the line, there's a sly little grin on her face. After all the jerks, Miss Kubelik has decided to trust this guy, just as at the end of *Breakfast at Tiffany's*, Holly decides to trust Paul. Miss Kubelik knows the way that life is; there is no time to mess around, so "Shut up

19. Palmer, "Healing the Heart" (lecture).
20. *The Apartment*, DVD, dir. Wilder.
21. Ibid.
22. Ibid.

and deal." When I call to schedule my next physical, apply for my next interim, or start a conversation with a disgruntled parishioner, I say my prayers and then I do it—I make my choice and hope for the best.

At the core of all these choices is my choice to follow the teaching of the psalm: "Commit thy way unto the LORD; and trust also in him; and he shall bring it to pass" (Psalm 37:5). I have chosen to make the commitment, and I am reaping great rewards. "They that sow in tears shall reap in joy" (Psalm 126:5). I have my life back, better than before.

In the very best and most deeply philosophical meaning of the term—think of William James and the American pragmatists—I have made a "pragmatic" choice for faith. I choose faith because it sustains my recovery from depression. I offer my recovery as proof of my faith. "Ye shall know them by their fruits" (Matthew 7:16a). Given all that faith has done for me, I would be crazy not to choose it.

There is an anecdote often told about Evelyn Waugh, author of books such as *A Handful of Dust* and *Brideshead Revisited*, that helps make my point. Nancy Mitford once politely asked Waugh how he could behave so miserably and still claim to be a practicing Catholic, indeed to be a devout convert. Waugh agreed with Mitford's assessment of his behavior and then said something like "You have no idea how much nastier I would be if I weren't a Catholic."

I'm not Waugh nasty. I'm Minnesota nice. But I admire Waugh's pragmatic spirit. His faith worked for him; mine works for me. It is helping to save my neck from depression. No, I can't tell you why there were Nazis or even how a can opener works. But I can tell you what gets me out of bed and allows me to do something productive. Early on, my Christian faith was called "the Way" (Acts 9:2). I am on the Way, and it is taking me where I much need to go to stay mentally healthy. To ask whether my faith is true is a nonsensical question. It's getting me where I need to go. And that is sufficient.

I had the good fortune of serving as an interim in a Minnesota prairie town, not far from the South Dakota border. One March morning I called a recently bereaved parishioner to schedule a visit. She lived ten miles or so north of town, too far to just drop in. "I don't know, Pastor. It's blowin' awfully hard. I can barely get the screen door open. If you come, be careful of the door."

I smiled; old people worry so much. I got directions and drove out to the place. There was a ground blizzard, where you can see the blue sky above, but the wind was whipping up the fallen snow so that you could barely see straight ahead. Her place was on the top of a little hill, just far enough north of town to be at the beginning of the glacial ridge. The fields around it were almost bare. The snow had all blown away. I got out of the car and walked up to the house with the wind at my back. I grabbed the screen door, which seemed to be stuck. I gave it a strong yank and the wind caught it, so that I had to hang on, not only for dear life but also to keep the door from sailing into the next county. Chalk up one for the weather wisdom of old ladies.

People, life, reality—I keep learning new things. It's fun. I do the best work I can with all the help I can get. At the same time, I can see the comic side of what I do. You should have seen me trying to hold on to that screen door. I'm a twice-broken person. I know how easily my life today could have been otherwise. Life is so good right now. I need someone to thank, and only God will do.

I have caught a glimpse of God in those who helped bring me out of my pit. I saw God in the face of a beautiful and kind Somali housekeeper. I saw God in the face of an elderly parishioner teaching me about reality out on the Minnesota prairie. Add my family, people I met in the hospital, many other parishioners, so many professionals who helped me, the authors of the laments, Dude, The Dude, and many more. They are my statement of faith. I can't do any better or be more honest. Besides, I don't need to.

I often think about what Anna told me my first afternoon in the hospital. "You know, Bob, my meltdown was the worst thing and the best thing that ever happened to me." Each day when I wake up and thank God that I want to get up, I am a little clearer about what she meant.

CHAPTER 13

A Pelican of the Wilderness

I

I hate myself.
> I am a worm, and no man;
I've let everybody down.
>> A reproach of men, and despised of the people.
>> Psalm 22:6

I've stopped making any sense.
> I am like a pelican of the wilderness:
I am insane.
>> I am like an owl of the desert.
>> Psalm 102:6

I can't make myself get of out bed.
> For my days are consumed like smoke,
I can't make myself do anything.
>> And my bones are burned as an hearth.
>> Psalm 102:3

My thoughts scream at me.
> I am weary with my groaning;
I can't sleep. I can't be still.
>> All the night make I my bed to swim.
>> Psalm 6:6a

I try to calm down, not to scream out loud,
> When I kept silence,
But I feel like my head is going to explode.
> My bones waxed old through my roaring.
> Psalm 32:3a

I bang my head repeatedly against the wall.
> Though thou hast sore broken us in the place of dragons,
I can't keep it together any more. I'm scared.
> And covered us with the shadow of death.
> Psalm 44:19

God, why don't you help me?
> Be not far from me; for trouble is near;
I'm a burden to everybody.
> For there is none to help.
> Psalm 22:11

God, don't you care about me?
> O my God, I cry in the daytime, but thou hearest not;
Why is this happening to me?
> And in the night season, and am not silent.
> Psalm 22:2

What is the point of going on?
> I am feeble and sore broken:
There is no point in living when all I do is hurt.
> I have roared by reason of the disquietness of my heart.
> Psalm 38:8

I just want it to stop now.
> My days are like a shadow that declineth;
I just want to die.
> And I am withered like grass.
> Psalm 102:11

A Pelican of the Wilderness

How easy it would be
    Why standest thou afar off, O LORD?
To drive my car into a tree.
    Why hidest thou thyself in times of trouble?
    Psalm 10:1

II

I'm taking matters out of your hands,
    I sink into deep mire, where there is no standing:
And putting you on a 72-hour hold.
    I am come into deep waters, where the floods overflow me.
    Psalm 69:2

O my God, what has happened to me?
    Let not the waterflood overflow me,
What will become of me now?
    Neither let the deep swallow me up.
    Psalm 69:15a

The nurse and the guard walked with me.
    And I said, Oh that I had wings like a dove!
The doors to the unit locked behind me.
    For then would I fly away, and be at rest.
    Psalm 55:6

My room is number 28.
    Yea, the sparrow hath found an house,
They'll keep my belt and dental floss at the desk.
    And the swallow a nest for herself.
    Psalm 84:3a

Do you promise not to hurt yourself tonight?
    Reproach hath broken my heart;
Take this. It will help you sleep.
    And I am full of heaviness.
    Psalm 69:20a

Are we feeling suicidal this morning?
>How shall we sing the Lord's song
I was in the loony bin.
>In a strange land?
>Psalm 137:4

I see my name in Dry Marker on the patient board.
>Keep me as the apple of the eye,
In the locked unit, they use only first names.
>Hide me in the shadow of thy wings.
>Psalm 17:8

III

A young man with a black T-shirt
>For he shall give his angels charge over thee,
Came and sat down next to me.
>To keep thee in all thy ways.
>Psalm 91:11

He said, "I don't know you. You don't know me."
>If I ascend up into heaven, thou art there:
"But we're all friends in here."
>If I make my bed in hell, behold, thou art there.
>Psalm 139:8

There are a lot of good people on the unit.
>By the rivers of Babylon,
We're like a family.
>There we sat down.
>Psalm 137:1a

Look, I'm not stupid. I've been through a lot of crap.
>Be ye not as the horse, or as the mule,
But there are people worse off than we are.
>Which have no understanding.
>Psalm 32:9a

I've got a purple pass and can go off the unit for an hour.
The LORD is my shepherd;
Can I get you something?
    I shall not want.
    Psalm 23:1

IV

I'm Bob. This is my first day in therapy group.
    I am counted with them that go down into the pit:
I'm diagnosed with major depression and anxiety disorder.
    I am as a man that hath no strength.
    Psalm 88:4

I'm a minister. I can't take the stress of my job anymore.
    My strength is dried up like a potsherd;
Right now, I can't even look after myself.
    And my tongue cleaveth to my jaws.
    Psalm 22:15a

"You'll need time to heal," the therapist said, "like after a heart attack."
    I waited patiently for the LORD;
You've gotten yourself into a corner. You need to turn around.
    And he inclined unto me, and heard my cry.
    Psalm 40:1

You're hurting and exhausted now.
    If I say, Surely the darkness shall cover me;
You will get better.
    Even the night shall be light about me.
    Psalm 139:11

"Bob," said the woman with the unicorn tattoo, "I'm glad you're here."
    He shall cover thee with his feathers,
"I thought ministers weren't real people."
    And under his wings shalt thou trust.
    Psalm 91:4a

V

My new friends had wristbands but no belts,
  For great is thy mercy toward me:
And they raised me up.
  And thou hast delivered my soul from the lowest hell.
Psalm 86:13

I've learned things I badly needed to know.
  They looked upon him and were lightened:
I messed up, but I am not a mistake.
  And their faces were not ashamed.
  Psalm 34:5

I've calmed down.
  Be still,
I don't need to be in control.
  And know that I am God.
  Psalm 46:10a

I can let things go.
  For a thousand years in thy sight
I've gotten some perspective.
  Are but as yesterday when it is past.
  Psalm 90:4a

I am no longer a perfectionist.
  For thou wilt not leave my soul in hell;
I know mistakes won't kill me.
  Neither wilt thou suffer thine Holy One to see corruption.
  Psalm 16:10

I am not ashamed of what happened to me.
  Create in me a clean heart, O God;
I am at peace.
  And renew a right spirit within me.
  Psalm 51:10

I've learned to face reality.
> Thou shalt tread upon the lion and adder:

I've learned to be an honest man.
> The young lion and the dragon shalt thou trample under feet.
> Psalm 91:13

I hurt so bad.
> Weeping may endure for a night,

I don't hurt now.
> But joy cometh in the morning.
> Psalm 30:5b

I *will never take happiness for granted again.*
> Bless the LORD, O my soul;

Thank you, God. Thank you for my life.
> And all that is within me, bless his holy name.
> Psalm 103:1

Resources

BIBLIOGRAPHY

Albom, Mitch. *Tuesdays with Morrie: An Old Man, a Young Man, and Life's Greatest Lesson.* New York: Doubleday, 1997.

Armstrong, Karen. *Twelve Steps to a Compassionate Life.* New York: Anchor Books, 2010.

Bellow, Saul. *The Adventures of Augie March.* Penguin Classics. New York: Penguin, 2006.

———. *Herzog.* New York: Penguin, 1976.

Borg, Marcus. *Speaking Christian: Why Christian Words Have Lost Their Meaning and Power—And How They Can Be Restored.* New York: HarperOne, 2011.

Bradshaw, John. *Healing the Shame That Binds You.* Deerfield Beach, FL: Health Communication, 1988.

Brown, William P. *Seeing the Psalms: A Theology of Metaphor.* Louisville: Westminster John Knox, 2002.

Brueggemann, Walter. *Israel's Praise: Doxology against Idolatry and Ideology.* Philadelphia: Fortress, 1989.

———. *The Message of the Psalms: A Theological Commentary.* Minneapolis: Augsburg, 1984.

———. *Praying the Psalms: Engaging Scripture and the Life of Faith.* 2nd ed. Eugene, OR: Cascade Books, 2007.

———. *The Prophetic Imagination.* 2nd ed. Minneapolis: Fortress, 2001.

———. *The Psalms and the Life of Faith.* Edited by Patrick D. Miller. Minneapolis: Fortress, 1995.

Burns, David D. *Feeling Good: The New Mood Therapy.* New York: Harper, 2009.

Chekov, Anton. *The Tales of Chekov.* Vol. 8, *The Chorus Girl and Other Stories.* Translated by Constance Garnett. 1920. New York: Ecco, 1985.

Clyde, Arthur, editor. *The New Century Hymnal.* Cleveland: Pilgrim, 1995.

Crouter, Richard. *Reinhold Niebuhr: On Politics, Religion, and Christian Faith.* New York: Oxford University Press, 2010.

Didion, Joan. *Slouching towards Bethlehem.* New York: Dell, 1968.

Eck, Diana L. *Encountering God: A Spiritual Journey from Bozeman to Banaras.* Boston: Beacon, 1993.

Gilbert, Elizabeth. *Eat, Pray, Love*. New York: Penguin, 2006.

The Holy Bible: Containing the Old and New Testaments, New Revised Standard Version. Nashville: Nelson, 1990.

Holy Bible in the Original King James Version. Gordonsville, TN: Dugan, 1988.

Kenyon, Jane. *Otherwise: New and Selected Poems*. St. Paul, MN: Graywolf, 1996.

Kierkegaard, Søren. *Purity of Heart Is to Will One Thing*. New York: HarperOne, 2008.

Kushner, Harold. *When All You've Ever Wanted Isn't Enough: The Search for a Life That Matters*. New York: Pocket Books, 1986.

Lane, Anthony. *Nobody's Perfect: Writings from the New Yorker*. New York: Vintage, 2003.

Lewis, C. S. *Reflections on the Psalms*. A Harvest Book. San Diego: Harcourt, 1986.

Martin, James, SJ. *The Jesuit Guide to (Almost) Everything: A Spirituality for Real Life*. New York: HarperCollins, 2010.

Melville, Herman. *Moby-Dick*. 1851. Reprinted, New York: Bantam Classics, 1981.

Moore, Christopher. *Fluke: Or, I Know Why the Winged Whale Sings*. New York: Morrow, 2003.

Norris, Kathleen. *Acedia & Me: A Marriage, Monks, and a Writer's Life*. New York: Riverhead, 2008.

———. *Amazing Grace: A Vocabulary of Faith*. New York: Riverhead, 1998.

———. *Dakota: A Spiritual Geography*. New York: Ticknor and Fields, 1993.

Palmer, Parker. "Healing the Heart of Democracy." Lecture, Westminster Town Hall Forum, Westminster Presbyterian Church, Minneapolis, April 19, 2012.

———. *Let Your Life Speak: Listening for the Voice of Vocation*. San Francisco: Jossey-Bass, 2000.

Peterson, Eugene H. *Answering God: The Psalms as Tools for Prayer*. San Francisco: HarperSanFrancisco, 1991.

Plath, Sylvia. *The Bell Jar*. New York: Harper Perennial, 2005.

Price, Reynolds. *Roxanna Slade*. New York: Scribner, 1998.

Rohr, Richard. *Things Hidden: Scripture as Spirituality*. Cincinnati: St. Anthony Messenger, 2008.

Solomon, Andrew. *The Noonday Demon: An Atlas of Depression*. New York: Scribner, 2003.

Taylor, Barbara Brown. *An Altar in the World: A Geography of Faith*. New York: HarperOne, 2009.

———. *Leaving Church: A Memoir of Faith*. San Francisco: HarperSanFrancisco, 2007.

———. *The Preaching Life*. Cambridge, MA: Cowley, 1993.

Tippett, Krista. *Einstein's God: Conversations about Science and the Human Spirit*. New York: Penguin, 2010.

———. *Speaking of Faith: Why Religion Matters and How to Talk about It*. New York: Penguin, 2007.

FILMOGRAPHY

The African Queen, DVD, directed by John Huston, 1952. Hollywood, CA: Paramount Home Entertainment, 2010.

All about Eve, DVD, directed by Joseph Mankiewicz, 1959. Beverly Hills, CA: Twentieth Century Fox Home Entertainment, 2008.

The Apartment, DVD, directed by Billy Wilder, 1960. Santa Monica, CA: MGM Home Entertainment, 2001.

The Big Lebowski, DVD, directed by Joel Coen, 2003. Universal City, CA: Universal Studios, 2003.

Blazing Saddles, DVD, directed by Mel Brooks, 1974. Burbank, CA: Warner Home Video, 1997.

Breakfast at Tiffany's, DVD, directed by Blake Edwards, 1961. Hollywood, CA: Paramount Home Entertainment, 2009.

Hannah and Her Sisters, DVD, directed by Woody Allen, 1986. Santa Monica, CA: MGM Home Entertainment, 2005.,

Independence Day, Blu-ray, directed by Roland Emmerich, 1996. Beverly Hills, CA: Twentieth Century Fox, 2010.

Now, Voyager, DVD, directed by Irving Rappe, 1942. Burbank, CA: Warner Home Video, 2001.

Rio Bravo, DVD, directed by Howard Hawks, 1959. Burbank, CA: Warner Home Video, 2010.

Rocky, DVD, directed by John Avildsen, 1976. Santa Monica, CA: MGM Home Entertainment, 2001.

The Shawshank Redemption, Blu-ray, directed by Frank Darabont, 1994. Burbank, CA: Warner Home Video, 2010.

Tootsie, DVD, directed by Sydney Pollack, 1982. Culver City, CA: Sony Pictures Home Entertainment, 2008.

Three Colors: Red, DVD, directed by Krzysztof Kiéslowski, 1994. New York: Criterion Collection, 2011.

The Untouchables, DVD, directed by Brian De Palma, 1987. Hollywood, CA: Paramount Home Entertainment, 2010.